"Why Didn't They Just Say That?"

Teaching secondary students with high-functioning autism to decode the social world using PEERspective

*An evidence-based practice:
Peer-mediated instruction and intervention*

Jennifer M. Schmidt, MEd

Foreword by Sean Barron

FUTURE HORIZONS

817.277.0727
817.277.2270 (fax)
info@fhautism.com (email)
www.fhautism.com

Publisher's Cataloging-in-Publication

Names:	Schmidt, Jennifer M., author. | Barron, Sean, writer of foreword.
	"Why didn't they just say that?" : teaching secondary students with high-functioning autism to decode the social world using PEERspective : an evidence-based practice: peer-mediated instruction and intervention / Jennifer M. Schmidt ; foreword by Sean Barron.
Title	
Identifiers:	ISBN: 978-1-942197-34-8; LCCN: 2017959252
Subjects:	LCSH: Youth with autism spectrum disorders--Behavior modification--Study and teaching. | Autistic youth--Behavior modification--Study and teaching. | Autism spectrum disorders--Patients--Behavior modification--Study and teaching. | Asperger's syndrome--Patients--Behavior modification--Study and teaching. | Social skills in adolescence--Study and teaching. | Social interaction in adolescence--Study and teaching. | Communicative competence--Study and teaching | Autism spectrum disorders--Patients--Life skills guides--Study and teaching. | Teachers of children with disabilities--Handbooks, manuals, etc.
Classification:	LCC: RJ506.A9 S36 2018 | DDC: 618.92/858832--23

Table of Contents

Acknowledgments

PEERspective was designed and implemented 10 years ago, so the thought of thanking all the people who've helped the program become what it is today is overwhelming. This new way of providing services to these often overlooked individuals is a true passion, and I am grateful for God's consistent calling on my heart to share it with the world. I will try to go through the last 10 years and list all of you; I'm sorry if I overlook including your name, but know I appreciate you all the same.

First of all, I have to thank my dear friend and colleague, Cindy Brinson, MA CCC-SLP, who helped design this class. This book and this class wouldn't have happened without you! Thank you for encouraging me and teaching me that it isn't always about the lesson plan. I am so grateful to have worked alongside you and blessed to be a part of Beavercreek City Schools.

Thank you to Marian West, my former principal, for allowing us to pilot this class back in 2007; you always believed we could make a difference in the lives of these amazing students and their parents.

Beavercreek is a wonderful place to call home, and there are so many people who have supported me and PEERspective, such as Jo Ann Rigano, Patricia Shannon, and my fellow Beavercreek City School employees, including Bobbi Fiori, BCS administration, and the BHS staff.

A special thank-you to Sara Anderson, M.Ed. Sara is a talented Beavercreek High School English teacher who has helped edit this book from start to finish. Thank you, Sara, for making my life's work make sense on paper. You helped shape my words without losing any of the meaning, and you were so fun to work with. I also owe a huge thank-you to Michaela Kramer, Ed.S., a school psychologist for Mason City Schools. Michaela worked tirelessly on helping create a strong research connection and helped with all the detail "stuff." I have learned so much from both Sara and Michaela through this process, and I'm grateful for their dedication, expertise, and friendship.

Over the past 10 years, my friends and family have probably heard more about PEERspective, my students, and this book than they'd like! I appreciate all the support, encouragement, prayers, and patience. Thank you to my parents, Bob and Karen Lee; my husband and best friend, Brad Schmidt; my daughters, Elyse and Corinne; my sisters. Rachel Siclari and Tricia Swallow; and my friends, especially Nicole Neal, Jill Bennett, Melaine Betz, Jackie Rock, Susan Myers, and Amy Mills. You have supported me through the ups and downs of the publishing process, and I'll always hold that close to my heart.

Sean Barron, my dear friend, took time to write the foreword to the book, for which I'm very grateful. But I have to thank Sean for much more. Thank you, Sean, for always providing me feedback about the class and my approach with my students. Through your life journey, you provide a perspective that is invaluable to me as a teacher and a person. I appreciate that you told me to "write the book like you are telling someone about the class." This piece of advice was the catapult to putting my words on paper.

Thank you to Julie Wilkinson, MA CCC-SLP, who teaches PEERspective at Centerville High School in Centerville, Ohio, and Jackie Anoleti, my former student teacher, for contributing lessons. Brenda Smith Myles and Kirsten McBride have been a joy to work with and have sculpted this project into what it is today. Lisa Combs, Heather Bridgman, and Carol Dittoe, thank you for answering my frantic novice author texts and for your continued support and kindness. You all are passionate, successful, and inspiring individuals, and your friendship and insight were invaluable.

Finally, thank you to my students and their parents, especially all of the student artists and Allison Kochensparger, who took most of the photographs included in the book. Past students have said that this class made a difference in their lives and helped them to "learn life," but really, you have made a difference in my life. You have shown me how to look at the world in a new way, how showing kindness hasn't gone out of style, and how to look outside the box. Last year, a student named Joe said, "My autism isn't a disease; it is a gift." I am eternally grateful that all of you have shared that gift with me.

– Jennifer Schmidt

Foreword

When I was only a few weeks old, my parents sensed something was profoundly wrong with me. I cried and screamed incessantly, made little eye contact, and could rarely be soothed or comforted. As young parents of their first child, they did everything in their power to address my needs and figure out why I was always frustrated and angry, while hoping my behavior was just a phase. But deep down, they knew better.

Things only worsened as I grew older. I was prone to inexplicable meltdowns and had a variety of sensory problems as well as speech and language delays before I finally received a diagnosis of autism in early 1967 when I was 5 years old. While my parents were temporarily relieved to know that my strange and unexplainable behavior was attributable to "something," the honeymoon was short-lived: Where do we go from there and from whom to seek help.

Receiving help for their deeply troubled child and working to break through my rigid ways of relating to my environment and others proved a daunting task. At the time, in the late 1960s, most of the experts in the field – and they were few and far between – were under the spell of Bruno Bettelheim, the Austrian self-educated psychoanalyst who became highly influential in the autism world, despite his dubious credentials, a trail of distortions and fabrications about his life, and no qualifications in psychotherapy or psychiatry. Nevertheless, Bettelheim, a Jew who had spent nearly a year in the Dachau and Buchenwald concentration camps in the late 1930s, was appointed to run the University of Chicago's Orthogenic School for disturbed children, where much physical and emotional abuse was said to have taken place.

Based on his experiences in the camps, Bettelheim apparently drew parallels between those with autism he had encountered and the surrounding prisoners of war, many of whom were listless and passive, made little eye contact, and seemed to have given up hope. He also extrapolated that the young people were autistic mainly because their parents – especially their mothers – were likely the equivalent at home of the cold, cruel guards at the camps, hence the "refrigerator mother" theory of autism. This was the framework under which Bettelheim operated and formed his core theories on autism, and before many of them were debunked, they had left a path strewn with emotional damage, unjustified blame, and heartache for many families. Even as recently as the early 1970s, most of the specialists who worked with my family made it clear that they felt, without saying it outright, that my mother was largely to blame for my unhappiness and misery.

That was then, and this is now.

Today, thanks largely to greater awareness and a shift from treating autism as a psychological malady to seeing it as a developmental condition, those on the spectrum have available to them many services, interventions, treatments, and strategies that were unimaginable a mere four decades ago. One of the most valuable of these, in my opinion, is the communications class Jennifer Schmidt has taught for 10 years at Beavercreek High School, which is the focus of this book.

Jennifer's curriculum pairs neurotypical students with students on the autism spectrum, which gives the former group numerous opportunities to bond with and help the latter, while further chipping away at the stigma that has surrounded autism for too long. She uses everything from movies to pop culture to her own experiences to foster in her students on the spectrum a deep understanding of and appreciation for the complicated nuances of social skills. When is it appropriate to tell a white lie as opposed to the brutal black truth? At the same time, her class instills in the students greater empathy and theory-of-mind concepts, both of which are highly difficult for many on the spectrum to grasp and internalize.

The instruction isn't confined to the four walls of the classroom. Jennifer also gives her students ample opportunities to apply their social-skills training in diverse settings, such as restaurants, movie theaters, and the local mall so they can cultivate successful interactions with others and build on them.

During a recent visit to her classes, I joined the groups for a scavenger hunt at a large shopping mall a few weeks before the Christmas holiday. The students were tasked with asking store employees for help in finding a number of items written on a list, which required them to make eye contact, use proper voice inflections, and overcome difficulties in approaching those outside of their comfort zone. Such experiences enhance their self-confidence while allowing them to construct a firm foundation upon which greater social-skills acumen can be built – and that will pave the way to greater success on the job, in relationships, and other areas of their lives.

Jennifer shared the story of a student I'll refer to as Mark, who was moved to her first communication class during the spring semester of the 2006-07 school year. When he entered her classroom, Mark was gloomy, refused to speak to his peers, made scant eye contact, and rarely lifted his head. After being exposed to Jennifer's caring attitude and deep compassion, which are part and parcel of her instruction, Mark's confidence slowly grew and "he felt less like a turtle," as Jennifer described it. Fast-forward to a few years ago, Mark earned his associate's degree from a local community college and went on to become a talented web designer and make many friends – all of which he largely attributes to Jennifer's communication class.

Jennifer is compassionate, energetic, humorous, and warm, and doesn't hesitate to go out of her way to work with her students' parents and guardians. She recognizes that they are an integral part of her curriculum's objectives, not separate from them. In recent years, she has become a sought-after speaker, presenting to educators and others on the critical value of incorporating social-skills training as well as its practical use and applications.

If Jennifer's communication class, also now known as PEERspective, had been offered when I was in middle and high school 40 years ago, would it have made a difference in my life? I can only speculate, but given my extreme difficulty in developing the ability to relate to others, my low self-esteem, demand for perfection, lack of perspective on what was and wasn't important in the big picture, and my overall self-loathing, I think I can safely conclude that it would have had a major positive impact on my development – in conjunction with everything my family was trying to do.

Formulating social skills, much like learning to play a musical instrument or a sport, is a process. No magic bullet has been invented to master it overnight. The many years it took me to learn these things were fraught with frustration, anger, and setbacks, all against a backdrop of limited acceptance and understanding of autism. Fortunately for many on the spectrum now, Jennifer Schmidt's teaching style, curriculum, and instruction as laid out here offer much more than fun times at the local mall and simple social interactions. They provide the solid blueprints for many young people to become happier and more successful and fulfilled adults. And isn't that what we all strive for?

– Sean Barron, author and freelance news reporter,
The Vindicator, Youngstown, Ohio

Sean has written or co-written the following:
- *There's a Boy in Here,* with his mother, Judy Barron (Simon & Schuster, 1992)
- *Unwritten Rules of Social Relationships,* with Dr. Temple Grandin (Future Horizons Inc., 2006, 2017)

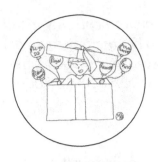

CHAPTER 1
A New Approach

"My autism isn't a disease, it's a gift." – Joseph

For far too long, we have looked at exceptionalities, such as autism, as a problem to be solved. When Joseph proudly announced that he was beginning to see his autism as a gift, I knew that the paradigm had shifted. Do people on the spectrum have to overcome challenges to find success in life? Sure, but don't we all? It's time we start shifting our thinking towards a new approach to intentionally teach these skills, and PEERspective allows us to do that.

Why is it that students with high-functioning autism (HFA) often see things differently than most of us? Every one of these students is unique, and everything I know about working with them I have learned because I messed it up a time or two – and they weren't afraid to tell me so!

After 20 years in the classroom, I am still learning, but in the process, I have made an important discovery: how to help students with HFA learn to better associate with their world. It is my hope that by sharing my experiences and class model, I am able to help others implement PEERspective in their schools. I am confident that this new approach will help your students start to decode the social world and eventually see their autism as the gift it can be.

Just because it makes sense, doesn't mean it's socially appropriate!

Once I discussed at length with a student, Dan, why it is not appropriate to pass gas in the middle of your advanced placement science class. After listening to me, Dan offered a rationale that I must admit made sense: "Passing gas is the body's natural way of expelling gas from the food we eat, and because I eat healthy foods I have more gas than most teenagers, who fill their faces with junk food."

I talked until I was blue in the face about how it smelled foul and how passing gas so obviously caused other students to think badly about him. I even went so far as to suggest him to blame the gas on the person next to him! I should have known that trying to persuade a student with HFA to lie wasn't going to work!

Frustrated, I decided to call in reinforcements: my friend, the speech-language pathologist, Cindy. Cindy brought Dan to her therapy room and continued the discussion of social thinking and etiquette. She even encouraged him to squeeze his "cheeks" together when feeling the urge to pass gas. Dan agreed that he would no longer publicly pass gas in his AP classes and that if he had no other options, he would at least do it more quietly, in the corner of the room.

One week later, an angry history teacher burst into my classroom, screaming, "Do you know what HE did now?!" I was afraid to ask, but did, and the teacher went on to explain that Dan had gone right up to her desk in the corner of the room, while she was seated there, and passed gas in her face.

Clearly, I had forgotten to include the critical advice to Dan that going to a corner to pass gas is only acceptable if there is no one sitting in the corner ... especially if that person is your teacher! While the teacher was understandably upset, Dan had actually done exactly what he thought he had been advised to do. Unfortunately, it had never occurred to me that I needed to teach not only the "Rule" but, just as important, the "Exception to the Rule."

Social Awareness Matters

Social awareness can make or break a person's success in life. The ability to interact in social, occupational, and academic settings is fundamental for positive social outcomes and the development of emotional maturity (Denham et al., 2001). Though they are often brilliant, many people on the autism spectrum are unable to obtain or maintain jobs due largely to their inability to understand social norms, often having difficulty understanding how to interact in social relationships (Myles & Simpson, 2001). In general, people don't lose jobs because they are incompetent; they lose jobs due to inappropriate use of social skills. Folkman (2013) found that employees who were let go typically had poor interpersonal skills and nobody to support them.

Without somebody to coach and guide employees on the spectrum, they are often written off after merely one or two poor social encounters. It is not good enough to be a technical genius; you have to learn to communicate as well. Students with HFA are often seen as rude and self-centered; lack of reciprocity and social awareness will do that to a person.

Social Implications

Along with the lack of reciprocity, most students with HFA have made many other social mistakes along the way, have probably written off friends or romantic relationships, and have almost always experienced bullying as a result of their lack of social awareness (Seaman, 2012). Close to half of all teenagers with an ASD are bullied at school, according to a 2012 survey of parents by the *Chicago Tribune* (Seaman, 2012). This is much higher than the estimated 11% of kids in the general population who are bullied (Seaman, 2012). According to a study by Humphrey and Symes (2010), students with ASD are approximately three times more likely to be victims of bullying than students with dyslexia (and students without identified disabilities). Furthermore, Humphrey and Symes (2010) found that students with ASD were the second most likely to be bullied, with students identified as having behavioral, emotional, and social difficulties being the most likely to be bullied.

Students on the spectrum are easy targets. Their encounters with bullying go one of two ways: either the student just looks down and ignores the bully, or he becomes the poster child for good vs. evil, causing him to insert himself into situations. Although well intentioned, I have known students with HFA to try to break up fights between teenage boys who were just rough-housing because they thought it was a real fight. After all, why would you pretend to fight with your friend? If you live in a black-and-white world, as do students with HFA, this does not make a whole lot of sense.

According to the *Diagnostic and Statistical Manual of Mental Disorders* (DSM-5; American Psychiatric Association [APA], 2013), autism is a pragmatic (social) communication disorder. Specifically, people with autism have deficits using communication for social purposes, impairments in the ability to change communication to match context, difficulty following the rules for conversation, and often cannot understand what is not explicitly stated. In addition, they are unaware of how their actions are perceived (Endow, 2016). The common impression that people on the spectrum do not care if people think they are rude is wrong. Instead, they sometimes appear that way because they are not able to automatically identify and use social information.

Social awareness and/or social interaction skills are critical to successful social, emotional, and cognitive development (Bellini, 2006). As educators, therefore, it is imperative that we teach pragmatic language to these students, who will not be able to reach their full potential in life if they are not taught how to play the "social game."

This all sounds great, but how do we teach social skills to students who are already in middle to high school?

Frustrated that the social skills that my SLP colleague, Cindy, taught in therapy and that I reinforced in my small-group tutoring class were not generalizing to the students' other classroom settings, we decided to brainstorm other approaches. In all fairness, we should not have been surprised at our lack of success, as research has shown that traditional social skills training programs are only minimally effective in teaching social skills to children and adolescents (Bellini, 2006; Gresham, Sugai, & Horner, 2001; Quinn, Kavale, Mathur, Rutherford, & Forness, 1999).

I had tried a "Lunch Bunch" type of group before, but it ended up becoming more like a social club where the students sat around and talked about "Dungeons and Dragons." While that was a good social outlet for some of my students with HFA, the students were not demonstrating, transferring, or generalizing the skills to other areas of their lives.

This time, we decided to try peer mentoring, also called peer-mediated intervention (Apple, Billingsley, & Schwartz, 2005; Bass & Mulick, 2007), whereby the teacher is more of a facilitator and nondisabled peers who have been systematically taught to prompt and respond to the targeted students become the teachers. Peer mediation is an effective strategy for facilitating social interactions with children with ASD, among other disabilities, and their nondisabled peers (Bellini, 2006; Laushey & Heflin, 2000; Odom, McConnell, & McEvoy, 1992; Sasso, Mundschenk, Melloy, & Casey, 1998; Strain & Odom, 1986).

I had used peers to facilitate social skills instruction and found this approach invaluable once rapport was established between the peers. So Cindy and I agreed that peer mediation was critical to our students mastering, transferring, and generalizing social skills for real impact in day-to-day life. However, we knew that we were missing a critical component to effectively teaching social skills: time! Gresham et al. (2001) recommended that social skills training be implemented more frequently and more intensely than is typically the case. They concluded that 30 hours of instruction, spread over 10-12 weeks, is not enough (Bellini, 2006).

We clearly needed to spend more time on social skills – 10 to 20 minutes a week were simply not sufficient in time and intensity to allow for mastery, and then generalization, of skills that are as complex and challenging for our students on the spectrum as chemistry or calculus might be to a neurotypical student. However, we were confronted with the challenges faced by most teachers: With ever-increasing demands for academic accountability along with dwindling resources, it is difficult to meet even the basic requirements of a modern secondary curriculum.

How could we make our ideas work? Cindy had an inspired idea: "Let's start a class." I loved the idea. We had to get approval from the administration, but suspected that they would see the need for such an intervention as much as we did. After all, they were "putting out fires" all day long with many of our students with HFA, and almost all of the perceived "behavior issues" really stemmed from pragmatic language deficits. Lack of social awareness and boundaries were usually to blame.

Undeterred, therefore, Cindy and I began to brainstorm our proposal to our building principal. We knew we wanted to keep the class fairly small, around 12-14 students. We wanted to create a class to include "targeted students" with HFA and "peer coaches." And we agreed that training the peer coaches about the characteristics of HFA was critical to our success.

As we discussed our proposed curriculum, we stumbled upon a Board-adopted human relations curriculum that aligned with the skills we had identified as being critical to teach, including topics such as trust/teambuilding, self-acceptance, stress management, anger management, nonverbal communication, dating, resolving interpersonal conflict, self-advocacy, and life transitions.

We felt that we could use the textbook adopted in the district, *Becoming Aware* (Walker, 2013), in our class for several reasons. First, it contained all of the topics that we wanted to cover; and second, it had already been approved by our Board of Education. Equally important, since it is a college-level textbook, it would present a challenging and respectful curriculum worthy of the academically gifted students who would be targeted for participation in the class.

Another important component of this new approach was one we felt was missing from most social skills training … authenticity. Discussion and role-play in a classroom can only go so far and are not the same as applying skills in the real world. Even when students know the steps in ordering food at a hamburger joint and can role-play the scenario in the classroom, for example, they tend to freeze up when having to do it in real life.

Research indicates that in order for social skills to generalize, or carry over into other areas naturally, they must be practiced in authentic settings (Radley et al., 2014). To address this issue of authenticity, we decided that each quarter we would require the students to attend one field trip during school hours and one social outing outside of school hours. All outings and field trips would involve authentic high school activities, occurring at football games, dances, restaurants, bowling alleys, movies, or the mall. This would allow students to practice the skills in authentic, natural environments. Prior to each outing and field trip we would discuss the event in detail and role-play different scenarios students might encounter.

Students enjoying their last field trip at Wellington Grille, a local restaurant.

Nevertheless, we anticipated that convincing academically gifted students to take a class taught by a special educator might be difficult; many of our students with HFA are very focused on getting their required classes out of the way, raising their GPA, and preparing for college. While social skill deficits are a detriment to any college student, this isn't always easy to explain to students or their parents.

Using a challenging college text would confirm to the students and their parents that this would not be a "special education" course, as the course content was something all the students might revisit in a commonly required college-level human relations course. Along with structuring our class around a respected text, we also felt it would be important for the students to earn credit for the class that would count towards graduation requirements. By granting credit, you entice not only the targeted students but also potential peer coaches. This allows your pool of possible peer coaches to grow significantly. If you don't offer credit, you will likely only get volunteers with extra room in their schedules who have empathy for students with special needs. While empathy is important, so is mutual respect. Students with HFA don't need a "helper"; they need a peer coach who will mentor them through the process of learning pragmatic language during the course of a year.

Finally, we decided that while I would be the lead teacher/teacher of record, Cindy would be my co-teacher. With my teaching background and Cindy's pragmatic language expertise, we felt that we would make a good team.

PEERspective

Cindy and I set up a meeting with our principal and the assistant principal who supervises our department. Presenting a formal proposal (see Appendix 3), we asked if we could pilot the PEERspective for one year, and explained that we would collect data using The Autism Social Skills Profile (Bellini, 2006) (see Appendix 1). After obtaining initial approval, we decided to meet again towards the end of our pilot year and discuss the data collected, as well as anecdotal evidence.

The results exceeded our expectations: It quickly became apparent that the social skills we focused upon began to flow over into the students' other classes. Other teachers were noticing that the targeted students became more confident and seemed happier. They were trying new things and making friends. The parents were also reporting on the difference they were seeing at home. Finally, one student said that after taking the class he felt "less like a turtle," able to come out of his shell and be a more active participant in the social world around him.

While we were thrilled we had found a way to help our HFA students, what we hadn't planned on was the lasting effect the class had on the peer coaches. They, too, gained confidence and assertiveness throughout the year, and seemed to benefit from the curriculum just as much as the targeted students. All students became friends over the course of the year, not because we told them to, not because they were being nice, but because they had the opportunity to get to know some outstanding people on the spectrum.

With a population whose pragmatic language skill gains are minimal, as evidenced in the educational literature, we felt that we were on to something, and that is how our model came about. We are delighted to be able to share the model with others, confident that this approach is effective and will make a difference in the lives of your HFA students as well.

PEERspective: Evidence-Based Practices

The PEERspective has proven to be an effective way of providing services to an underserved population. The combination of time, intentionality, peer models, authentic practice, and other evidence-based practices (EBPs) is what makes the PEERspective work. In an effort to determine which interventions are most effective for students with ASD, the National Professional Development Center on Autism Spectrum Disorders (NPDC) applied a set of rigorous criteria to a series of interventions commonly used with this population of students. Twenty-seven interventions met the criteria as being effective with students with ASD when implemented correctly NPDC, 2011.

PEERspective incorporates 21 out of the 27 EBPs, so it is no surprise that huge improvements are being observed in the performance and behaviors of participating students with HFA, both inside and outside of school. The following table lists the EBPs that are part of the program, along with their definitions.

Evidence-Based Practice	Definition (NPDC)	How EBP Is Used in PEERspective	Rationale
Antecedent-based Interventions	Includes stimulus control in which environmental modifications are used to change the conditions in the setting that prompt a learner to engage in an interfering behavior. The goal is to identify factors that are reinforcing the interfering behavior and then modify the environment or activity so that the factor no longer elicits the interfering behavior.	PEERspective teaches students strategies to help them modify the environment so as to ease sensory sensitivities. Environmental factors include, but are not limited to, lighting, noise levels, schedule changes, and overcrowding.	By modifying environmental factors such as lighting, noise levels, and other sensory-related elements, students can focus on academics and are better prepared to modify the environment in their future lives.
Cognitive behavioral interventions (CBI)	Based on the belief that behavior is mediated by cognitive processes, this group of interventions emphasizes teaching individuals to monitor and manage their own thoughts, feelings, and behaviors.	CBI are embedded in several lesson plans in PEERspective, but are specifically used when teaching about filtering thoughts and feelings and using a "thought bubble."	Students will be more successful in life if they effectively manage their feelings and filter their thoughts based on the setting, audience, and relationship.
Computer-aided instruction	Consists of the use of computers to teach academic skills and to promote communication and language development and skills. It includes modeling appropriate skills and behaviors and providing competent tutors.	The use of computers, smartboards, and other types of technology occurs at least weekly in PEERspective.	Using modeling and computers creates buy-in and allows students to see the skills and concepts being taught.
Developmental relationship-based treatment	Involves a combination of procedures that are based on developmental theory and emphasize the importance of building social relationships.	Unit 1 in the PEERspective model is Trust and Teambuilding. This is the framework for constructive peer mentoring and social relationships throughout the year.	The targeted students and the peer coaches must trust each other so they can open up and try new things. Honest, open friendships are a vital part of PEERperspective.
Exercise	Involves an increase in physical exertion as a means of reducing problem behaviors or increasing appropriate behavior.	PEERspective uses exercise throughout the year, in various lessons. Unit 4, Managing Stress and Wellness, focuses on the importance of exercise through the practical exam.	Allowing students to try different types of exercise can help them realize the benefits by actually feeling the difference before and after, which can make it more concrete and create buy-in to incorporate daily exercise for better mental and physical health.

Evidence-Based Practice	Definition (NPDC)	How EBP Is Used in PEERspective	Rationale
Extinction	Used to reduce or eliminate unwanted behavior that involves withdrawing or terminating the positive reinforcer that maintains an interfering behavior. The subsequent withdrawal results in stopping or extinguishing behavior. The interfering behavior is likely to increase in frequency and intensity (extinction burst) before it is extinguished as learners try to elicit the reinforcers previously provided. Often used with differential reinforcement.	PEERspective coaches are taught to ignore inappropriate behavior or redirect social behavior that is out of the norm for their peer group and demographic.	By ignoring or redirecting inappropriate social behavior, targeted students learn what is and isn't acceptable. Attention-seeking behavior is reduced or eliminated because social skills are taught intentionally rather than being ignored.
Functional communication training	Systematic practice to replace inappropriate behavior or subtle communicative acts with more appropriate and effective communicative behaviors or skills. First the interfering behavior is analyzed to determine its communicative function through functional behavioral assessment, and then a replacement behavior is taught to take its place.	Capitalizing on teachable moments is an important part of successful social skills intervention. Peer coaches help to determine which behaviors are not appropriate socially, and through role-play and discussion, an alternate behavior is taught.	Often students on the autism spectrum (targeted students in PEERspective) don't realize their behavior is socially unusual. Most students with HFA are very open to learning what is appropriate and will work hard to replace previous inappropriate behavior with support.
Imitation-based interaction	Interventions that rely on adults imitating the actions of a child.	Drama and role-play are used throughout PEERspective.	Imitating the peer coaches using role-play of upcoming events and then practicing these skills in authentic settings helps the skills generalize.
Modeling	Interventions in which an adult or peer demonstrates the target behavior for the learner to imitate. Often combined with other strategies such as prompting and reinforcement.	Drama and role-play are used throughout PEERspective. Peer coaches are trained to be models both in and outside the classroom.	Students learn social skills by watching their peers. Targeted students and coaches create a trusting relationship, which allows the modeling to occur naturally, thereby enabling the targeted students to "see" what is appropriate social behavior.
Naturalistic intervention (NI)	Collection of practices, including environmental arrangement, interaction techniques, and behavioral strategies, used to promote appropriate communication and social skills. These practices encourage specific target behaviors based on the learner's interests and build more elaborate learner behaviors that are naturally reinforcing and appropriate to the interaction.	PEERspective utilizes NI in the classroom every day, as well as in the school community and in field trips and outings throughout the year. This is also fostered through the extracurricular club (Social Communication Club) that is connected closely with PEERspective.	In order to generalize, social skills must be practiced in authentic settings such as classrooms, the school community, as well as on field trips and other outings.

Evidence-Based Practice	Definition (NPDC)	How EBP Is Used in PEERspective	Rationale
Peer-mediated instruction and intervention (PMII)	Involves teaching typically developing peers ways to interact with and help children and youth with ASD acquire new behavior, communication, and social skills by increasing social opportunities within natural environments. PMII is also a useful strategy for promoting positive transitions across settings. Peers are carefully and systematically taught strategies for engaging children and youth with ASD in positive and extended social interactions in both teacher-directed and learner-initiated activities.	Peer coaches are same-age peers who have been trained to work with students with HFA. This is one of the most important components of PEERspective.	Students learn more quickly from their same-age peers than from adults.
Prompting	Procedures include any help given to learners to assist them in using a specific skill. Prompts are generally given by an adult or peer before or as a learner attempts to use a skill. Prompting procedures that have been shown to be effective with learners with ASD include least-to-most-prompts, simultaneous prompting, and graduated guidance and can include verbal, gestural, and model prompts.	Peer coaches are trained in when and how to prompt their peers in various settings. The teacher or therapist who is teaching PEERspective is also consistently prompting peer coaches and targeted students throughout the school year both during and outside of class.	Many students on the spectrum don't realize when a behavior is inappropriate or how to communicate effectively. Prompting allows these students to learn these skills in real time and provides an alternative approach for the future.
Reinforcement	If a consequence increases the probability that a behavior will occur again, it can be said to be a reinforcer. Positive reinforcement involves offering incentives to reward behavior. An example of positive reinforcement is a token economy. Negative reinforcement involves removing an aversive stimulus to reward behavior so that learners will use the targeted skill or will not engage in interfering behaviors.	Peer coaches and teachers/therapists use reinforcement as a teaching tool throughout the school year.	Pointing out when a student is showing social growth is an important part of the learning process. Positive feedback is a powerful reinforcer, especially when given by a respected same-age peer.
Scripting	Involves developing a verbal and/or written script about a specific skill or situation, which then serves as a model for the child with ASD. Scripts are usually practiced repeatedly before the target skill is used in an actual situation.	Upcoming social events and/or social interactions may warrant the use of scripting. This is usually created jointly by the student, the teacher/therapist and, most important, the peer coach.	By scripting out upcoming social situations and role-playing them, the students on the spectrum can approach an event with more confidence.

Evidence-Based Practice	Definition (NPDC)	How EBP Is Used in PEERspective	Rationale
Self-management	Interventions that help learners learn to independently regulate their own behaviors and act appropriately in a variety of home, school, and community-based situations. With these interventions, learners with ASD are taught to discriminate between appropriate and inappropriate behaviors, accurately monitor and record their behaviors, and reward themselves for behaving appropriately.	Unit 5, Conflict Resolution, is an intentional way of teaching self-management skills. "Thought bubbles" and theory of mind are also underlying themes in PEERspective.	In order to have successful peer relationships and future job success, students must learn to manage their thoughts and behaviors.
Social narratives	Interventions that describe social situations in some detail by highlighting relevant cues and offering examples of appropriate responding. They help learners adjust to changes in routine and adapt their behaviors based on the social and physical cues of a situation, or are used to teach specific social skills, communication skills, or behaviors. Social narratives are individualized according to learner needs and typically are quite short, perhaps including pictures or other visual aids.	This strategy is usually used one-on-one with the teacher/therapist and the student on the spectrum. On occasion, a peer coach is involved. Social narratives can incorporate a cartoon-type framework to illustrate social skills visually.	Social narratives are effective in creating a visual interpretation of past or future social situations.
Social skills groups	Social skills groups are used to teach individuals with ASD ways to appropriately interact with typically developing peers. Social skills groups typically involve small groups of two to eight individuals with disabilities and a teacher or adult facilitator. Most social skill group meetings include instruction, role-playing or practice, and feedback to help learners with ASD acquire and practice communication, play, or social skills to promote positive interactions with peers.	PEERspective is a social skills group but on a larger scale, because it is taught every day. The Social Communication Club is an extracurricular club that complements PEERspective and is based on the format of social skills groups.	Social skills groups have proven effective and can be a stepping stone toward implementing PEERspective community that could be future peer coaches or targeted students.
Task analysis	The process of breaking a skill into smaller, more manageable steps in order to teach the skill. Other practices, such as reinforcement, video modeling, or time delay, can be used to facilitate acquisition of the smaller steps. As smaller steps are mastered, learners become more independent in performing more complex, including physical or routine tasks (e.g., self-care, work tasks), as well as academic, behavior, communication, play, social and transition related skills.	Task analysis is used throughout the school year in PEERspective, especially with upcoming social events such as school dances, field trips, outings, or other school events.	Task analysis is a way to help ease anxiety about upcoming events, for example, by creating a step-by-step framework.

Evidence-Based Practice	Definition (NPDC)	How EBP Is Used in PEERspective	Rationale
Time delay	Focuses on fading the use of prompts during instructional activities (A brief delay is provided between the initial instruction and any additional instructions or prompts.) Has been demonstrated to be effective with skills in the academic, communication, play, and social domains.	Time delay is naturally used by teachers/ therapists and peer coaches by fading prompts and "coaching" throughout the year.	Peer coaches are taught to guide only as needed and to not do anything for a student that the student can do him/herself. The goal is for students to naturally do most social things independently by the end of the school year.
Video modeling (VM)	Uses video recording and display equipment to provide a visual model of the targeted behavior or skill (typically in the behavior, communication, play, or social domains). Types of video modeling include basic video modeling, video self-modeling, point-of-view video modeling, and video prompting.	Video modeling is used often in PEERspective, as a whole class, in small groups, and individually. Role-play can be recorded and then viewed and analyzed. Many of the lesson plans in this book utilize video VM as indicated at the bottom of the lesson plan outline.	VM is a powerful tool and is used in PEERspective as often as possible. Students on the spectrum are able to replicate appropriate social behavior and interaction if they can see themselves and/ or others doing it effectively.
Visual supports	Involve any tool presented visually that supports an individual as he or she moves through the day. Applicable to many skill domains, visual supports might include, but are not limited to, pictures, written words, objects within the environment, arrangement of the environment or visual boundaries, schedules, maps, labels, organization systems, timelines, and scripts. They are used across settings to support individuals with ASD.	In PEERspective many visual supports are used. These include, but are not limited to, visual timer, consistent location of the date, plan for the day. and announcements. as well as any schedule changes. Handouts are created for many lessons in this book as visual aids.	Students on the spectrum are often visual learners and prefer consistency and predictability. Visual tools help provide these supports, and are easy to implement in any classroom setting.

Based on NPDC (2011).

This book is your step-by-step guide to implementing PEERspective in your district, or at the very least allow you to start intentionally targeting social skills through the lesson plans provided. While the lesson plans are designed for high school students, they can be modified for a variety of grade levels, settings, and ability levels. In Chapter 2, we will look at the steps involved in implementing PEERspective into your setting with ease.

(Opening art) Mackenzie said she felt really nervous when she started PEERspective this year, but after just 5 weeks she reports feeling "relaxed, calm and confident." This is an extra special year because not only do I have amazing students like Makenzie in my class, my oldest daughter, Elyse, is a peer coach this year. She's been going on social outings with my students since she was 5 years old, so having her in class is surreal.

CHAPTER 2
Course Design

"Do I look like I have a particle accelerator in my back yard?" – Aaron F.

There are many ways to look at and solve a problem. One day in class, Aaron responded to a question about a viable way to deal with a troubling issue in his life with this rather far-fetched idea. While the coaches and I decided to talk him out of this approach, it did make us all wonder (a) what in the world a particle accelerator was and (b) how that could possibly help?

As you plan to implement PEERspective at your school, the following questions will help guide you in the initial design of the program:
- What kind of credit will students earn for participating in the class?
- How long will the course be?
- Who will be teaching the course?
- In what other ways can we incorporate social skills training into our school?

Each school is unique, so you will have to work with your administrators to discover what delivery methods are the best fit for your students and school environment. In this chapter we will discuss how we addressed the above questions as we initially designed the PEERspective in our school.

Credits

As mentioned earlier, it is essential for students to earn credit for participating in the course. Students are more likely to buy into the lessons if the class is earning them not only a grade, but also a credit towards their graduation requirements; furthermore, you want to attract academically minded peer coaches along with establishing buy-in from the students on the spectrum and their parents. If the class does not hold academic value for all involved, it is not seen as a priority to the students or parents.

How Long Is the Course?

The class can be offered as either a semester (half of the school year) or yearlong course. Each session is an entire class period, which in my high school lasts 50 minutes. Whatever length you choose obviously impacts not only how much content you can cover, but also the type of credit your school will offer. The guidelines for teacher qualification requirements and class coding vary from state to state, so you will need to work with your administrators in order to navigate these realms. These credit offerings and class codings are dependent upon who teaches the course and in what subject he or she is certified.

Who Will Teach the Course?

While staffing in your school or district will play a large role in the approach you choose, the benefits of co-teaching the class versus having just one teacher should weigh heavily into the final decision. In the pilot year and for several years afterwards, our class was co-taught by me, a special education teacher, and a speech-language pathologist (SLP). In my opinion, this is the preferred delivery system. That is, the SLP looks at things through a therapist lens, whereas the special educator is trained as a teacher. These two points of view can be a powerful combination both inside the classroom and in planning for lessons and writing data-driven IEP goals (see Appendix 2).

When a special educator and an SLP co-teach, the traditional speech pull-out setting is integrated with a resource room/general education setting. This is the ideal setup; however, SLPs are often spread very thin and may not be able to balance their pull-out therapy with co-teaching. If this is the case, it is still recommended that the therapist help plan and come to class as much as possible. For example, I recommend that the SLP attend class on a consistent schedule so that the students are expecting her and are not distracted by her presence. I also recommend that the SLP teaches lessons at times and does not pull students out of PEERspective for any individual therapy. This type of arrangement in students' junior or senior year can be a stepping stone towards dismissing students with HFA from speech and language services, meaning they no longer need to be pulled out of their general classes for individualized instruction.

While co-teaching is optimal, in the real world, what is optimal sometimes isn't an option. Currently, I am lead teaching the class with consultative services from our SLP. The SLP travels between three buildings each day and has many students on her caseload, and she simply cannot carve out enough time to co-teach or co-plan. In addition to coming into class a few times a week to observe, discuss progress, and consult as needed, she also follows up with the students' general education teachers, which allows us to see if the practiced skills are generalizing. We also find time to jointly evaluate the collected data and write IEP goals.

Teaching Social Skills Across the Curriculum

While it would be ideal for every school to offer intensive social skills intervention through PEERspective, this may not be plausible. If your school is not in a position to start a semester or yearlong class, there are still a number of ways to integrate social skills lessons into various disciplines with the help of peer models, and perhaps if you are able to show growth through these easily implemented strategies, you could propose piloting your own class.

Social skill training is important in any classroom setting to help students develop *social competence* – the ability to engage in social interactions, establish and maintain relationships, and communicate needs and wants across contexts (Merrell & Gimpel, 1998; Stichter, Randolph, Gage, & Schmidt, 2007). Students who do not demonstrate social competence may be at risk for peer rejection, academic failure, social dissatisfaction, and poor social perception (Alwell & Cobb, 2009; Sherman, Rasmussen, & Baydala, 2008). They may also experience negative long-term outcomes, such as difficulty developing relationships, maintaining employment, and a lack of outside interests (Eaves & Ho, 2008; Stichter, Conroy, & Kauffman, 2007).

Research has revealed a positive relationship between self-efficacy and success (Bandura, 1977a, 1993; Mills, Pajares, & Heron, 2007; Zeldin, Britner, & Pajares, 2008). Thus, providing opportunities for students to be successful in social interactions, both in and out of the classroom, is a positive step toward improved social skills training. Just by having students work collaboratively on projects or lessons, you are fostering social communication. When students are allowed and encouraged to take chances, they can, and eventually will, overcome their fears and become confident, as they begin to see that they can experience positive social interactions if they push themselves beyond their comfort zone and take a chance. Since students on the spectrum tend to be visual learners, positive social memories can cultivate confidence and generalize into others areas of their lives. That is, if students can "see" or remember themselves having successful social interactions, they will be more likely to do it again.

In any discipline, you can require students to present their work to the rest of the class, individually, in pairs, or in groups. I usually start the year having students present in groups, then progress to presenting in pairs, and then require individual presentations by the end of the year. Furthermore, in any subject area, playing games is an easy and fun way to get students to interact and socialize. Games can be relevant to the curriculum or stand alone as a reward for positive behavior, etc. I do a few "Game Days" throughout the year, where students are allowed to play games of their choosing; the only rules are that the game must be approved by the teacher and that everyone must be actively participating.

Games teach turn-taking, empathy (through taking on others' perspective), sportsmanship, teamwork, compromise, and a multitude of other life skills that are vital to effective social interaction and eventually job success (Fenaughty, 2014). When you let students play games, they may think you are just being nice by allowing them to have fun, but in reality, they are practicing essential social skills that will benefit them beyond the classroom.

Social Communication Club

Teaching and practicing social skills does not only have to occur within the hours of the school day. Student clubs are yet another way to foster positive communication skills.

John, a PEERspective student, came into my room for lunch one day, as he did every day. This day was different, however, as it was blatantly obvious that John had something on his mind. The first clue was that he wasn't stimming as he usually did, and the second clue was that he had forgotten to buy his lunch. As he paced back and forth near my desk, he asked me what the protocol [was] for implementing a club.

As I answered, he told me that I would need to be the advisor of his still unmentioned club, because I was "an obvious choice." Right as I was letting him know that I couldn't add anything more to my already full plate, he shared his idea for the Social Communication Club (SCC). He explained that he wanted to start a club where people could "practice their social skills and hang out and talk about nerdy things." Even if my schedule was already full, there was no way I could to tell this amazing individual no – not only was this a good idea and a wonderful complement to PEERspective, it was amazing to witness him making this heartfelt proposal, which must have been really hard for him.

Thanks to John, SCC now meets once a month from September through May. The first meeting provides a brief overview about autism and the purpose of the club. Then, we brainstorm what social outings we want to do each month. For example, we might go on a hay ride in October and have a Thanksgiving dinner in November, go holiday shopping in December, and so on. Students serve as club president, vice president, and secre-

Participants in the Social Communication Club (SCC), a school-sponsored club.

tary, send out reminders, and plan the outings, which is great socialization practice for them and makes leading the group much easier for me.

The club has grown over the years to include 35-40 students. While I always encourage the PEERspective students to be a part of the club, it is not a requirement. SCC outings enable students to interact with other students they know from class, while also meeting new people. Furthermore, they allow students who have already taken the class to continue to practice their social skills with friends. Besides, it is a way for me to get to know freshmen and sophomores who may be future candidates for PEERspective.

Leading such a club may be a precursor to starting PEERspective or, at the very least, allow you to provide authentic social practice where all students can experience positive social interactions beyond the confines of the school day. However, before these things can occur, you have to get your administration on board. That process is outlined in Chapter 3, so keep reading!

(Opening art) Artwork for this chapter was created by Tad. Tad was recommended as a student artist by my friend, who works in the library. Tad wasn't enrolled in my class, but he joined us on some outings because his girlfriend was in the class. When choosing targeted students, it is important to seek recommendations from staff and general/advanced teachers because not all students with HFA come with paperwork!

CHAPTER 3

Getting Administrators and Parents on Board

"I was feeling adventurous, so I ordered brown bread." – Aaron L.

I am blessed to be able to have my room open to students at lunchtime. This allows students a chance to escape the craziness that is a typical school lunchroom. One day, a student came in to eat with his friends from PEERspective. Aaron always bought his lunch, which was usually the same thing on any given day of the week. But on this particular day, as he entered the room, he proudly announced, "I was feeling adventurous, so I ordered brown bread!" While at first glance, this doesn't seem earth shattering, it was a big deal for Aaron – he was learning to branch out and try new things.

It's time for you to order your own "brown bread." PEERspective is your opportunity to try a new way of offering social skills training to students with HFA. Nothing worth doing is ever easy, but in this chapter we have done the legwork for you. In addition to the steps outlined below, you will find all relevant materials in the appendices: sample proposal for your administration (Appendix 3), sample syllabus (Appendix 4), data collection methods and suggestions (Appendix 5), and letters to parents inviting their son or daughter to participate in your class (Appendix 6).

Step 1: Getting your administrator's approval.

Students who do not understand the social world can unintentionally end up in the office. Many administrators struggle to help these students and their parents understand the implications of these visits. While autism awareness is often at the forefront of the news, school personnel, while well intentioned, may or may not be prepared to work effectively with these students and their parents.

Our proposal for our social skills class was simple, yet thorough, outlining our plan with data to support implementing the class. As you begin planning your proposal, you may find it helpful to find out how many students with ASD your school and/or district serves. (This information is available through the data collection system your state uses, which is reported by your district.) In addition to these figures, you might ask your school's SLP for a list of students who would benefit from the program. We also suggest you ask fellow teachers, both special and general educators, because some targeted students may not have disclosed a disability, but could still benefit from inclusion in your class. To help you with the task of identifying potential students, Appendix 5 includes a checklist you can ask teachers to fill out to identify students.

After you have identified students who will benefit from the class, you need to plan your approach. We started with one class period (50 minutes every school day), and I suggest that is where you should start, too. Next, you need to decide on the delivery model you will use; will you co-teach with an SLP or are you going to do it alone?

As you continue to prepare your proposal, be sure to include the importance of field trips and outings so the students can practice skill generalization. Administrators are less hesitant to approve field trips if you explain their importance. (To keep the cost to the district low, we only ask for transportation costs from the district and require the students to pay for the cost of the field trip, such as entrance fees, a meal, or a game of bowling. Most parents are very supportive of our efforts and do not mind this minimal expense.)

Another critical component of your proposal is the curriculum/syllabus (see Appendix 4), which allows your administration to get an idea of the type of class you are proposing to teach. PEERspective can be mistaken for a special education course. Although the class is taught by staff from the special services department, the curriculum is not special education. Targeting students who are in general to advanced classes and using a textbook and curriculum that is used at the college level is a selling point for this course. If your district has a human relations curriculum, I highly advise you to look at it. You may find that the topics you want to teach (highlighted in later chapters) align with the human relations curriculum.

After you have completed these steps, you should feel confident that you have a strong proposal to submit to our administration for their approval.

Step 2: Send a letter to parents.

After you have received your administration's approval, you are ready to begin! The first step here is to send a letter of invitation to parents of potential student participants (see Appendix 6 for sample letters – one for targeted students and one for the peer coaches). It is important for parents to know exactly what the class is designed for and why their child has been chosen. Most parents and students are thrilled to be part of our program.

Once you have the class approved and students lined up, you are ready to begin changing your school for the better! A checklist of all the steps is included in Appendix 7.

(Opening art) Sam designed the artwork for this chapter after much convincing. Sam wus in PEERspective during the 2013-2014 school year, and then he was my student aide during the 2014-2015 school year. He is one of the most musically gifted students I have ever had the privilege to work with.

CHAPTER 4
Key Components of PEERspective

"Takeaways are like theorems in math!" – Isaac

At times, my students fixate on the details and miss the application of a lesson. Take-aways are big-picture ideas that students can take (away) from a lesson and use in their lives. One day, a student, Isaac, had an epiphany and consequently blurted out, "Takeaways are like theorems in math!" Upon some investigating, as math isn't my strongest subject, I learned that theorems are formulas that have been proven true, so I think his analogy is correct. Now that's a takeaway!

In this chapter, we will look at seven components of PEERspective that are critical to the success of the program: peer modeling, field trips and social outings, book talks, takeaways, the classroom environment, journaling, and parental involvement.

Peer Modeling

Peer modeling is the most essential part of the program. Imitation is an early skill that serves an important cognitive and social function in typical development (Uzgiris, 1981). As such, we learn social skills by observing others, mimicking their actions, and then making these skills a part of our repertoire (Bandura, 1977b). While neurotypical (NT) students often do this with ease, most students on the spectrum fail to notice the social world around them and, therefore, miss out on this essential skill building.

Another factor leading to students with HFA not picking up effective social cues may be genetic (Risch et al., 2014). If students with ASD spend the bulk of their time with people who also struggle with social-emotional development, even if they are paying attention, they are not picking up on effective approaches to socialization.

Further, by the time students are eventually motivated to learn these important life skills, they are often older and have been the victims of bullying (Hebron & Humphrey, 2014). Beyond the obvious effects of having encountered bullying, students with HFA also tend to mistrust their peers – sometimes justifiably so. So, we are left with motivated students who don't have the opportunity to learn these skills because they are not traditionally taught in school. Besides, these students don't trust their peers so they don't typically observe and learn these skills. This is why PEERspective is so important; this approach provides an intentionally safe and effective way for students to master life skills that will serve them now and in the future.

One aspect of PEERspective that has proven to be vital is the use of same-age peers. Peer-mediated instruction is one of the 27 evidence-based practices for autism intervention (NPDC, 2011) mentioned in Chapter 1, and forms the major underpinning of PEERspective. My students don't want a 42-year-old woman teaching them how to ask someone on a date; they want advice from their peers who have gained their trust throughout the year. Peer coaches are often the best teachers in the room on any given day.

But much more is involved than just letting the students watch their NT peers. Given the importance of peer modeling, it is essential to ensure that the peer coaches are appropriately trained. To prepare them for the critical role they will be playing in PEERspective, the coaches attend a one-day session in the summer, usually the week before school starts. The goal of this session is to teach the basic characteristics of ASD and train the students in how to be good peer coaches. See Appendix 8 for an example agenda; by visiting (peerspectivelearningapproach.com), you can also view video modules designed to assist in effectively training peer coaches.

As part of their training, it is important for the NT peers to understand that they are "coaches," not "helpers." Semantics matter, and no student with a genius-level IQ is going to buy into having a "helper." During the training (see sample agenda in Appendix 8), coaches are taught about the symptoms and implications that are often associated with ASD and how they can coach the targeted students through modeling and assertive but kind redirection. They also hear from past PEERspective participants – both coaches and students with ASD – as well as from parents of previous participants, to help them understand how important their role is and how this class can impact their own lives. They participate in a simulated activity about how it feels to have ASD, and they are treated to lunch so they can begin to build rapport with each other even before the school year begins. Finally, I explain the structure of the class and remind them that not only are they coaches/mentors, they are also taking the class and earning a credit towards graduation.

Field Trips and Social Outings

Without practice in authentic settings, students are rarely able to use the social skills they have learned in other settings without prompting and intervention (Bellini, Peters, Brenner, & Hopf, 2007; Ganz et al., 2012; Rao, Beidel, & Murray, 2008; Yakubova & Taber-Doughty, 2013). Since the goal is for students to be able to use these skills in their other classes, in the community, and at their future colleges and places of employment, practicing their skills in authentic settings is essential.

Field trips. Within PEERspective, field trips occur once a quarter during school hours. The skills students will be using during these events are intentionally taught ahead of time, and are observed and redirected during the event. In addition, following the field trip, the class "debriefs" about how the authentic practice went. For example, in December we visit the mall, a typical hangout for high school students around the holidays, to practice social skills through a scavenger hunt activity; a sample questionnaire is included (Appendix 9).

The informational scavenger hunt is designed to take the skills we have worked on in class and encourage skill generalization. The students are broken into groups of two, one target student and one coach. I usually let the students have input about who they want to work with, but I keep the pairing intentional and do not broadcast why the students are paired in a certain way. As a result of their training, the coaches understand that if I allow students to choose a partner to work with, they are to choose a target student.

The pairs then navigate the mall, asking questions at various stores. They take turns asking the sales clerks the questions, which have been provided ahead of time, and they coach each other throughout the activity. For example, if one student did not make eye contact and the clerk, therefore, did not know that he wanted to ask a question, his partner could point that out so the student will remember to do so the next time. The two students take turns asking questions that require information that cannot be found on a sign or around the store, and record the answers on their questionnaire to earn points.

After the pairs complete the scavenger hunt, we all meet at Santa and take a picture, which the students get to keep. Why? Well, many of my students have never been to the mall with their friends. It is important for these students to have positive social experiences, or they will be less likely to put themselves out into the social world again. More than that, it helps them to think outside the box a little more, because while it may not seem age-appropriate to have their picture taken with Santa, high school students do this all the time for fun with their friends. Admittedly, this is a grey area because if a high school student did this alone, it would generally not be considered socially appropriate, but with friends it is. During the field trip debriefing, this issue lends itself to a great discussion. Plus, it can be fun to be silly. Being silly is not something most students with HFA participate in with friends either!

Other potential field trip ideas include an etiquette lesson at an upscale restaurant, lunch at a casual restaurant, mini-golf, bowling, or any other common high school activity that can allow the students to practice socialization.

Social outings. Social outings follow a structure similar to field trips, but happen after school hours. Many of my students with ASD have never been on social outings with peers, and they have to push themselves outside their comfort zone to attend. Because of the growth they experience throughout the class, often by the end of the school year they are not only attending outings with ease, but many students begin to participate in additional outings with friends and even host their own parties.

For an outing in the fall, we generally attend a school football game together. Once, following this outing, a former student, Levi, shared,

"I was very scared to attend the first outing because it was a football game. Mrs. Schmidt provided me with earplugs, and I ate a lot of snacks and talked to my friends from PEERspective. The cheerleaders came over and cheered just for us and threw us towels. I have been to every football game since. I didn't know I liked them because I was too scared to go."

Levi illustrates that you don't know if you like something until you try it. Nevertheless, many of the students end up deciding that they don't really like to attend football games, and that is fine; the goal is to allow them to experience a typical high school outing, not to convince them to like football. Also, this outing allows them to see that even if they didn't like the football game, they still can feel proud of themselves for going. This social confidence and shared experience cracks open the door to trying out the social world a little at a time.

Jarrett and Hannah look on as Brandon celebrates his strike at a bowling field trip.

Outings can be any event that allows students to gather beyond the school day; other ideas for potential outings include attending sporting events or plays, going to the movies, going shopping, attending school dances, or going to gatherings hosted by students. These shared experiences help to continue to build rapport and show students that the risk of putting themselves out there can end in friendships and acceptance.

Book Talks

Another way to help students have a shared experience and similar things to discuss is through Book Talks. While the image of middle-aged moms at Starbucks discussing novels might come to mind, our version of Book Talks is teenagers sitting at their desks arranged in a circle, discussing a book and enjoying a hot beverage – but with a grade attached. The students really enjoy this activity, and it allows them to learn about social situations in a nonthreatening way, all while sharing their opinions and observations as they feel comfortable. (See the Book Discussion Log in Appendix 10.)

Students are given class time to read their novels, and on book discussion days, they are allowed to bring in baked goods, while I provide coffee, tea, and hot chocolate. Students are divided into pairs, and are responsible for grading each other's participation (see form in Appendix 11). You can vary the requirements, but I usually have each student share one question or comment, one takeaway, and one quote from the book. The partner setup allows the peer coaches to help prompt their partner, along with allowing the target students to see a model of how to meet the requirements by watching their partner. Book discussion days offer a relaxed change of pace from the day-to-day curriculum.

Book selection. We have approached Book Talks in a number of ways. In the past, our former school librarian helped us choose popular young-adult titles that tied into the themes of the course. If you want to approach book talks in this manner, some potential titles to consider could include:

Theme: Anger, Trust and Managing Feelings
- *Whale Talk* by Chris Crutcher
- *Iron Man* by Chris Crutcher
- *Staying Fat for Sarah Byrnes* by Chris Crutcher

Theme: Interpersonal Relationships
- *Sleeping Freshmen Never Lie* by David Lubar
- *Strays Like Us* by Richard Peck
- *Among Friends* by Caroline B. Clooney

Theme: Human Rights, Tolerance, Self-Disclosure
- *A Child Called It* by Dave Pelzer
- *I Know Why the Caged Bird Sings* by Maya Angelou
- *Bad Boy: A Memoir* by Walter Dean Myers

Theme: Life Transitions, Decisions, Dating
- *Tuesdays With Morrie* by Mitch Albom
- *Eleanor & Park* by Rainbow Rowell

While we have used some of the above titles as a subtle way to spark conversation, currently we use Michelle Garcia Winner's *Socially Curious, Curiously Social* (2009). This book gets right to the heart of what we are teaching, which is theory of mind (TOM) – the ability to understand and identify the thoughts, feelings, and interactions of others (Baron-Cohen, Tager-Flusberg, & Lombardo, 2013).

Takeaways

Takeaways, or ideas that students can take from a lesson and use in their lives, have proven to be very helpful in driving home the "big picture." By ending a lesson and/or unit by focusing on the takeaway, the students understand how our lesson and experiences in class can have a lasting impact on their lives. This is similar to using "exit tickets" to assess and obtain information about student's current levels of understanding a learning (Marzano, 2012).

A good example of takeaways occurs in the self-awareness unit (see Chapter 6), where the students take a *Myers-Briggs Type Indicator®* (Myers, McCaulley, Quenk, & Hammer, 1998/2003) personality test online, read about their personality, and then work in groups with students who have similar personality types. While I want students to know how their personality type has an impact on how they relate to others, and that there are certain strengths and weaknesses associated with their personality type, there is a much bigger picture to this unit – the realization that everyone is unique and that we all struggle in some areas and excel in others. I also want students to take away the fact that if we are aware of our weaknesses, we can modify our natural behavior and prevent them from negatively impacting our life, so we focus on this as the takeaway from the activity.

Many students on the spectrum lack TOM, which, in turn, adversely affects their interpersonal relationships and social interactions (Stichter, O'Connor, Herzog, Lierheimer, & McGhee, 2012). That is, they are often unable to see how their words and actions impact those around them. If you don't realize you are being perceived as rude or mean, you are not able to change your behavior to get the desired outcome.

Over the years, countless students have some up to me, saying, "Why didn't they just say that?" after misreading a subtle social cue and learning the intended meaning. Most students I have worked with over the years do not get their feelings hurt easily and appreciate honesty. Once the students start to grasp TOM, they can use this knowledge to adjust some of their behaviors and keep some thoughts and comments safely locked away in their "thought bubble." Use a Comment Card (Appendix 12) to assist you in this; some of our students think that they have to say whatever pops in their heads, and teaching the skill of Not Talking can be of great use to them in the future. The use of a "thought bubble" has also proven effective because it's a visual representation of something figurative. By putting a name and picture in a "thought bubble," many students have reported being able to "see" their thoughts in the bubble instead of actually saying them. This is obviously a very important skill in high school and in the future.

By filtering their thoughts and actions and utilizing TOM, students start to implement self-management, which is another recognized evidence-based practice (NPDC, 2011). By learning self-awareness, they are better able to monitor their behavior and make changes and adjustments as needed.

These "big-picture ideas" are often lost on students with HFA, who tend to be detail-orientated and fixate on specifics (APA, 2013). When taking the personality test, they may find it interesting to learn that they scored high in a certain area and that certain strengths could lead to a career in engineering, for example. However, the real lesson here is the broad implications on their life and their social relationships. We need to teach students to think in new ways and understand that we don't all think in the same way, and takeaways can do just that.

Classroom Environment

As educators, we strive to provide a comfortable learning atmosphere where all students can feel safe and learn. Below are some ways to do that.

Visual supports. Among the many ways to accomplish this for students with ASD, Koul, Schlosser, and Sancibrian (2001) note that "clinicians and educators need to utilize a wide range of intervention strategies that can take advantage of visual modality in individuals with autism" (p. 166). Visual stimuli can be used to teach a variety of social skills and provide students with concrete choices without having to rely on linguistic recall (Alberto, Cihak, & Gama, 2005; Bates, Cuvo, Miner, & Korabeck, 2001; Cihak, Alberto, Taber-Doughty, & Gama, 2006). For example, I use a board to post schedule changes and list the daily lesson plan every day, and employ a visual timer to aid students during activities.

While these ideas may not seem groundbreaking, these types of visual supports – yet another example of an effective EBP (NPDC, 2011) – can help students with ASD, and most students, feel secure by providing structure and thereby lessening uncertainty and the anxiety that often comes with that.

Sensory issues. Another way to create a positive classroom environment is to pay attention to the ambience of the room. Children with ASD tend to have hyper- and/or hypo-sensory responses to stimuli around them (Kientz & Dunn, 1997; Myles, Mahler, & Robbins, 2016), and such atypical sensory processing can have a negative impact on their functioning. For example, fluorescent lighting, which is common in many schools, can be bothersome to students from a sensory standpoint. Add in the fact that dress codes often prevent students from pulling their hoods up or wearing hats to shade their eyes, and it is easy to see that lighting can create a sensory problem. If you cannot change or modify the lights, you may consider placing individual lamps around the classroom instead of the overhead light, or simply turning on only one set of lights. Simple changes like this can have a large impact on creating a comfortable classroom environment.

> *Although sensory interventions are not identified as an EBP, antecedent-based interventions are! If you modify lighting in your classroom, you are using an antecendent-based intervention.*

Journaling

Journaling is another key component of PEERspective. Journaling is typically done at the beginning of the class period; sometimes the journal prompt is to get the students thinking about the upcoming lesson, at other times it is just to allow them to get something out of their heads. Regardless, journaling can be a helpful practice for students to process their thoughts by putting them on paper.

Journaling is also a way to integrate cognitive behavior intervention (CBI) (NPDC, 2011) into the class. CBI utilizes so-called cognitive restricting, which includes modifying how one thinks, feels, and behaves in order to improve social and behavioral outcomes. This, in turn, allows students to become more aware of themselves and others, which can lead to improved social interactions and social confidence (Hart & Morgan 1993; March & Mulle, 1998; Reaven & Hepburn, 2003).

In PEERspective, journaling is followed by optional sharing time. As such, it can lead to some great teachable moments that would have been lost in the shuffle of my well-thought-out lesson plans, as illustrated in the following.

One day a student, Jeremy, came into class, all confused about being invited by a girl to the homecoming dance. He wrote in his journal, and shared his journal entry with his peers. He reported that the girl had asked him out in one of his advanced classes and that he was flustered, and had told her that he would have to ask his mom and get back with her. Ouch!

I didn't know the girl. However, the peer coaches did, and said that she had been dating someone for a long time, and was known to be "less than kind." The peers talked to Jeremy about the situation and how to handle it, including never saying he had to check with his mom, under any circumstances, ever.

The next day, when the girl asked Jeremy about the dance, he simply replied that he had gotten a better offer. She looked silly, and he was now more aware that, sadly, the social world around us isn't just confusing, it can also be harsh. Thankful for his friends' advice, Jeremy ended up attending the dance with a group of PEERspective students. What could have been a situation that caused him to never want to attend a dance or speak to a girl again ended well because of his friends, the peer coaches.

Parental Involvement

While we don't want older students to admit to "asking their mom," parents nevertheless play a large part in supporting students, and parental involvement can be an important catalyst for success in PEERspective. Often, parents of students on the spectrum are worried about "forcing" their children to attend social outings. This is understandable because many times, these students have had negative social experiences over their life span. One parent told me that she had hosted two or three birthday parties where no one came, so they started just going out to dinner with family on her son's birthday. This is not acceptable, provided the student really wants a party with same-aged peers. All students have a lot to offer friends, and no one should host a party where nobody shows up.

I usually wait until about a month into the school year to hold a parent meeting, so that the students have started to make friends and talk about the class at home. These parent meetings always yield positive results. At the very least, it is good for the parents to meet each other. More important, though, they learn about the program as I explain the structure of the class and discuss the importance of outings and field trips, emphasizing how these events help the students to push themselves outside of their comfort zones. I also reassure the parents that I will be at the events, and that the students are only required to come and try. If a student decides to leave early, I just applaud her for trying, as do the other students. As the year progresses, students tend to stay at outings longer and begin to enjoy going to school the next day and discussing their shared experience.

It is important to understand that parents are often just as nervous as their children about embarking on something new like this. We need to remember that they are entrusting us with their care. Citing research about the importance of authentic practice for social skill generalization can be a helpful addition to this meeting (Timler, Vogler-Elias, & McGill, 2007). In order to swim, you must first dip one toe into the water, so any involvement is a step in the right direction. Having parental support is an essential tool to help students start learning to swim through the world of social interaction.

(Opening art) One of my favorite memories of the student artist of this chapter (Danielle) was when she attended prom. Her PEERspective friends helped her pick out a dress and decide how to do her hair and makeup for the big night. Then a classmate asked if his mom could come in and help Danielle "accessorize" because she worked for a home jewelry company. I was proud of Danielle for pushing herself outside of her comfort zone, but I was equally impressed with her friends for their love and support.

PEERspective CURRICULUM

UNIT 1:
Trust and Teambuilding

"PEERspective is a breath of fresh air." – Alaina

The atmosphere in any classroom isn't simply defined by the purposeful setup and thoughtful lessons plans; it's also the feeling you get when you walk into the room. Often students who struggle socially have never experienced the feeling of being accepted and celebrated at school. By creating a foundation of mutual respect and acceptance right from the start, PEERspective often becomes a safe haven for all students and a refreshing break in their day.

It's no accident that trust and teambuilding are the first topics we cover, as these themes are embedded in many lessons throughout the course. Interacting with others is something we can "force" someone into. But we cannot "force" the target students and peer coaches to become friends. Friendships take time to develop. What we can do, however, is spend time focused upon building the foundation for friendships, and that is, therefore, an essential aspect of a successful class.

The friendships that evolve over the course of students' time together are built on mutual respect, shared experiences, intimate conversations, and purposeful cooperative learning. I'm proud to say that many students remain friends beyond high school.

A former peer coach, Airius Moore, is now an out-of-state college football player who doesn't get much time off, so his breaks are limited and precious. However, when back in town, Airius makes it a point to meet up with a friend he made during his time as a peer coach. Arius said, "In PEERspective, I made a lot of friends and met a lot of people, but I made the biggest connection with Yaseen. Yaseen and I talk from time to time, and when I'm home we usually play video games and talk about sports. Lately though, we have been talking about college, since he will be making that transition next year." Not only did Yaseen make a friend through PEERspective, he made a lasting friend who is mentoring him through the next stage of his life and likely beyond.

These types of relationships are not fabricated or forced; they happen when people are given the opportunity to be themselves and allow others to get to know them. When students begin to have social success, their confidence increases, and they become more willing to push themselves to try new things and make even more friends, so coaching our students through trust and teambuilding exercises is a vital part of the class.

Sadly, many students with ASD have had negative experiences trusting their peers. The rates of bullying among students with ASD are staggering. For example, a recent study conducted by the Interactive Autism Network (IAN) found that 63% of students ages 6 to 15 with ASD had been bullied at some point in their lives (Zablotsky, Bradshaw, Anderson, & Law, 2014). While people seem to be understanding and accepting when someone has an obvious disability, unfortunately, this is not so for students with HFA. You don't get a free pass when you are in mainstream classes messing up the curve on every test, as many of my students do, or answering every question in the review game.

According to the book *The Global Achievement Gap* (Wagner, 2008), seven skills for the 21st century promote future success for students. These historically underestimated skills include critical thinking and problem solving, collaboration across networks and leading by influence, agility and adaptability, initiative and entrepreneurialism, effective oral and written communication, accessing and analyzing information, and curiosity and imagination. These vital life skills are interwoven into PEERspective units and lessons, helping prepare brilliant minds to shape and change the future and will be noted prior to each unit.

The Amazing Race was designed and implemented by Patrick, who was a peer coach in PEERspective and also a National Honor Society member. His NHS service project included stops during the race with fun challenges, as pictured here.

While Unit 1 focuses specifically on trust and teambuilding, many of the lessons in this unit lend themselves to be integrated throughout the year. Building rapport is not just a first-quarter goal; it is something that is continual and can happen in many unique ways. For this unit, we study Chapter 6, "Developing Close Relationships," of *Becoming Aware* (Walker, 2013), which includes information on topics such as the development of relationships, becoming friends, dating and mate selection, communication problems, codependence, and other concepts relating to relationships, friendships, marriage, and family.

Specific lessons include:
- Trust walk
- Goal setting
- All about me pictures
- Service learning exploration
- How can we make a difference?
- Let's make a difference!

Survival Skills for the 21st Century Used in This Unit

Critical thinking and problem solving, collaboration across networks and leading by influence, agility and adaptability, initiative and entrepreneurialism, effective oral and written communication, accessing and analyzing information, and curiosity and imagination.

(Opening art) I couldn't resist using another of Tad's drawings. Tad graduated last year and is now attending a local college majoring in engineering. Tad is dating my current student, Grace, who reports that they have been dating for "one year, four months, and 12 days."

Unit 1: Trust and Teambuilding
Lesson 1: Trust Walk

Materials

- Planned walking route that is safe and accessible
- Blindfolds (1/pair)
- Reflection handout (Unit 1, Handout 1)

Duration

One 50-minute class period

Lesson Overview

The students are divided into pairs (one coach and one target student). Students take turns being blindfolded and leading each other on a walk. (If students are not comfortable being blindfolded, they may close their eyes instead.) Students can verbally give directions and/or hold the other person's hand/arm in order to safely navigate the walk. This is not a timed activity, and the students should be instructed to go at a speed that ensures that the blindfolded student is comfortable and safe at all times.

Student Objectives

1. The students will rely on each other to complete the task. Because this task cannot be completed alone, students begin to build trust.

2. The students will effectively communicate to their partner what speed and direction they need to go in order to avoid bumping into other pairs and/or obstacles that may be in their way.

3. Prior to starting this activity, the students will discuss a strategy that allows both partners to feel comfortable.

Rationale

During the course of PEERspective, the students will need to trust each other. They will need to know that the other person will help them get through situations both inside and outside the classroom. They will also learn that often a task cannot be completed on their own. In order to learn from each other, there must be a mutual respect, which is built on trust and shared experiences. This activity provides both of these essential components.

NPDC Evidence-Based Practices Used in This Lesson

- Developmental relationship-based treatment
- Peer-mediated instruction

Trust Walk

Partner #1:_____ Partner #2:_____ Date:_____

Pre-Walk Discussion Points

Discuss your strategy for this activity with your partner. Be sure to talk about how you are feeling and what approach would make you most comfortable. What will be an effective but comfortable way to complete this activity? (Remember: There is no time limit.)

What strategy did you agree on?

How are you feeling prior to this activity?

Post-Discussion Question

Do you feel your strategy was effective? Would you change anything if you were to do this activity again? How are you feeling after completing this activity?

Unit 1: Trust and Teambuilding
Lesson 2: Goal Setting

Materials

- SMART Goal brainstorming sheet (Unit 1, Handout 2)
- Note card or decorative paper to write final goal (can be displayed in the classroom or kept private)
- 1 copy of *Oh, the Places You'll Go* by Dr. Seuss (1960)

Duration

One 50-minute class period

Lesson Overview

The students work individually to create social goals for the year. These goals may or may not align with their IEP goals. The students create the goals, and they do not have to share them.

Start by reading aloud to the class *Oh, The Places You'll Go* by Dr. Seuss (1960) and discuss the importance of goal setting. Emphasize how essential it is to include certain components when creating goals; we use SMART goals: Specific, Measurable, Attainable, Realistic, and Timely (Doran, 1981). Share this acronym and give examples of goals that fit the formula and goals that do not. For example, "I'm going to get into shape" doesn't fit the SMART goal formula, but "I am going to run a 5K in three weeks" does fit the formula. For social goals, "Make friends" isn't going to work, but "Invite one friend over to my house during each quarter" is SMART. After learning about SMART goals, allow students to brainstorm potential goals together.

Student Objectives

1. The students will learn the SMART goal formula.

2. The students will learn how to write attainable and measurable goals.

Rationale

Students will have more ownership and motivation to meet a goal they consider valuable. By allowing students to brainstorm potential goals in small groups, they see that all of us have things we want to improve in our lives. Teaching them how to write SMART goals will allow them to understand that the criteria involved in writing these goals are important.

NPDC Evidence-Based Practices Used in This Lesson

- Cognitive behavior intervention
- Prompting
- Reinforcement
- Visual supports

SMART Goals

Name:_____Date:_____

SMART goals are:

Specific

Measurable

Attainable

Realistic

Timely

Brainstorming: Write your ideas for possible SMART goals below.

(Adapted from Doran, 1981)

Unit 1: Trust and Teambuilding
Lesson 3: All About Me Pictures

Materials

- Blank paper, one sheet for each student
- Markers, colored pencils, and/or crayons

Duration

One 50-minute class period

Lesson Overview

Each student is given a piece of blank paper and drawing utensils such as markers, colored pencils, or crayons. Students write their name in large letters in the middle of the paper. Around their name, they draw or write 20 things about themselves. This may include a sport they play, food they like, favorite book, number of people in their family, etc. Upon completion, the students individually present their pictures, which are then hung in the classroom for the remainder of the year. By displaying these pictures, a sense of community begins, and visual reminder of peers' names and interests are always available.

Student Objectives:

1. The students will begin to get to know each other.

2. The students will begin to learn each other's names and have a visual reminder of each classmate's name and interests.

3. The students will begin to discover shared interests and characteristics.

4. The students will present their paper to the class and by doing so begin to push themselves outside of their comfort zone.

Rationale

This activity encourages the students to begin to get to know each other. It is important for the students to begin to make connections with their peers because friendships are often built on common interests and experiences. It is also important for all of the students to know each other's names. This activity provides a visual reminder of names and interests and can aide in knowing what to talk about with their peers.

NPDC Evidence-Based Practices Used in This Lesson

- Developmental relationship-based treatment
- Visual supports

Unit 1: Trust and Teambuilding
Lesson 4: Service Learning Exploration

Materials

- Journal*
- Pens or pencils

*Please note: Each student is asked to bring in a composition notebook at the beginning of the year, as it will be used frequently through PEERspective. This is also stated on the sample syllabus.

Duration

Two 50-minute class periods with home assignment

Lesson Overview

Each student interviews a relative, teacher, or other trusted adult who is a volunteer and donates time or talents to a charitable organization in their city, state, or country. In pairs (one target student and one peer coach), the students brainstorm during class to make a list of questions for the interview. Then, on their own, the students conduct the interview and record the answers in their journals. Finally, students summarize and present their findings to the class and share what they learned.

Student Objectives

1. The students will use communication skills to develop interview questions using the WH-word guide (who, what, when, where, and why).

2. The students will independently set up and conduct an interview outside of class with a trusted adult regarding a charitable organization the person is involved with.

3. The students will record answers and share what they learned with the class.

4. The students will work together to compile a summary of their findings about volunteer opportunities.

Rationale

In order to become comfortable participating in conversations, the students must become more aware of the relationships around them. They also have to evaluate what is important to themselves and others and compare/contrast their values and opinions. In this lesson, they will utilize their skills by conducting a one-on-one interview and then presenting to the class. Finally, they will record their findings in their journals and use this information for the next lesson on how to make a difference.

NPDC Evidence-Based Practices Used in This Lesson	
• Cognitive behavioral intervention	• Peer-mediated instruction and
• Developmental relationship-based treatment	intervention
• Naturalistic intervention	• Scripting

Lesson contributed by Julie Wilkinson, MA, CCC-SLP, Centerville High School, Centerville, OH.

Unit 1: Trust and Teambuilding
Lesson 5: How Can We Make a Difference?

Materials

- Student journals
- Pens or pencils

Duration

One 50-minute class period

Lesson Overview

After conducting interviews with trusted adults about a charitable organization (Lesson 4), the students work together as a class to decide how they can make a difference in their community by volunteering their time, money, or items to the organization of their choice. After brainstorming ideas in their journals, students agree on one organization to help.

Student Objectives

1. The students will discuss which organizations are meaningful to themselves and to the people they previously interviewed.

2. The students will compromise by choosing one organization to help.

Rationale

In order to work effectively on a team with others who have different opinions and backgrounds, the students must become more aware of their own communication and social skills. They will have to listen to others' opinions, evaluate the opinions/information, and finally compromise to make a decision. It is important to allow enough time for each student to state his/her findings, answer questions, or research information.

NPDC Evidence-Based Practices Used in This Lesson

- Cognitive behavioral intervention
- Developmental relationship-based treatment
- Naturalistic intervention
- Peer-mediated instruction and intervention
- Scripting

Lesson contributed by Julie Wilkinson, MA, CCC-SLP, Centerville High School, Centerville, OH.

Unit 1: Trust and Teambuilding
Lesson 6: Let's Make a Difference!

Materials

- Student journals
- Pens or pencils

Duration

Three or more 50-minute class periods (depending on the chosen service project)

Lesson Overview

After choosing a charitable organization to help, the students begin to implement a team service project. First, the students or the teacher invite a representative from the organization to visit the classroom; prior to the visit, they prepare a list of questions in their journals to aid in deciding the specifics of their service project based on what they learned from the guest speaker. After the visit, they decide on the project and create a timeline towards accomplishing their goal.

Student Objectives

1. The students or the teacher will invite a guest speaker.

2. The students will work together to develop interview questions prior to the visit.

3. The students will use communication skills to conduct the interview and begin to "think on their feet" about asking additional questions that may surface.

4. The students will use planning/organizational skills to set a service goal/timeline.

Rationale

In order to become comfortable talking to people they do not know; the students must plan ahead and write a list of questions for the interviewee. They will also have to listen to the answers and develop additional questions as the interview progresses.

NPDC Evidence-Based Practices Used in This Lesson

- Cognitive behavioral intervention
- Developmental relationship-based treatment
- Naturalistic intervention
- Peer-mediated instruction and intervention
- Scripting

Lesson contributed by Julie Wilkinson, MA, CCC-SLP, Centerville High School, Centerville, OH.

Additional Activities and Ideas for Unit 1

NOTE: Many of the following activities and ideas are also applicable to other units.

- **Ice Breakers:** In order to trust each other and function as a team, it is essential that students come to know each other. Ice breakers are a simple way to build rapport and can be used at any point in the unit or year. Simple name games, "two truths and a lie," and a variety of other activities that require students to work together and/or share about themselves can be effective tools in working to build trust and community in your class.

- **Class Shirts:** Many clubs and sports teams use "spirit wear" as a way to demonstrate camaraderie and a sense of belonging. Each year, as a class, we develop a shirt that can be worn on field trips, outings, to special events, or on selected days. The design process may be a collaborative decision with all students giving input and coming to consensus, or students may submit designs from which the class members vote on their favorite. This is an authentic way to start teaching compromise and what it means to be part of a group. However, this can be challenging for students who lack perspective-taking skills (Fisher & Happé, 2006), so we preface the activity with a discussion about compromise, listening skills, and the importance of saying things in a polite way. I usually do this activity about a month into the school year so the students know each other better and are more willing to respect their peers' opinions.

- **Classroom Jobs:** Giving the students specific jobs allows them to take leadership roles and become important parts of the class. Students may act as treasurer, secretary, and photographer/historian; for example, the secretary and treasurer handle the orders and money for our class t-shirts, whereas the historian documents our events throughout the year. I like to find jobs that fit with students' natural talents. For example, this year we have a videographer – a peer coach who wants to study videography – who creates videos documenting some of our activities throughout the year. He posts these videos online so the students can show their family some of the things they have been involved in during PEERspective. Classroom jobs can be filled by both target students and peer coaches and can encourage the students to work as a team.

- **Service Learning:** Service learning is often overlooked as a way not only to teach empathy but also to enhance the teambuilding you are already doing in class by providing a shared experience and sense of accomplishment found by helping others. Participating in a community provides members with opportunities to share information, gain knowledge, develop relationships, and problem solve (Morrison & Blackburn, 2008). Community building can foster definition, structure, and provide the support many students with autism require for learning, practicing, and generalizing social behavior (Aspy & Myles, 2016). As an example of service learning, our class volunteers at a 5K run that is held in a former student's honor. We pass out t-shirts and race packets, do walk-up registration, cheer for runners and walkers on the route, and hand out water and snacks.

Service learning is invaluable for all students; it is an effective way to show students that there are lots of caring people in the world and that reaching out to help others can actually be just as beneficial to you as it is to them. This intangible feeling is hard to capture and even harder to teach.

- **Competitions:** Any opportunity for students to work together on a project leads to team-building and trust among the peers. Our students work in groups on seasonal projects such as a pumpkin carving competition, a gingerbread house activity, school-sponsored door decorating contests, or an egg decorating contest, and even an Amazing Race around town (with parent drivers). I have even used 100+ piece puzzles and timed the groups to see who could put the puzzle together the fastest. These types of activities teach teamwork and also allow students opportunities to see that others' way of thinking may be beneficial in solving a problem and that their own way is not always the only way or the best way – a hard lesson for many students on the autism spectrum to learn.

UNIT 2:
Self-Awareness, Self-Acceptance, Disclosure

"Your face is so … symmetrical." – Jesse

One day, a student of mine was trying to give a genuine compliment, but all he could comment on was the symmetry of Carly's (a peer coach) face. While we chuckled at his unexpected delivery, Jesse was making progress towards increased social awareness by even attempting a compliment. The coach was quite gracious as she just thanked him and probably began to look at her reflection in a whole new way.

While one of the goals of PEERspective is to help students become more socially aware and learn when to adjust their behavior to their surroundings, it is also important to help students accept themselves. Students need to see themselves as unique and valuable. Seeing their uniqueness as a gift, coupled with increased social intelligence, can help build confidence and a better quality of life for students with HFA.

After spending time establishing trust and building rapport in Unit 1, in Unit 2, we embark on a self-discovery process. In order to be able to advocate for their needs and adjust behavior that may be unknowingly pushing people away, students must become more self-aware. Many of our students do not have a good self-awareness and often do not feel good about who they are. Although some of their natural tendencies, such as intense interest in a certain topic to the almost exclusion of anything else, might be perceived as odd and unexpected, they should still be celebrated. Barry Prizant, in his book *Uniquely Human*, states that, "Autism isn't an illness. It's a different way of being human" (Prizant & Fields-Meyer, 2015, p. 4). According to Prizant, there is no such thing as autistic behavior. These are all human behaviors and human responses based on a person's experiences. In other words, we all have certain things that we find stimulating – it's just that students on the spectrum often take it to a whole new level.

Helping students manage their interests and unique behaviors is something we focus upon in PEERspective. As this email from a fellow educator demonstrates, figuring out how to help accomplish this is not always easy.

Jen,

I realize that you are probably very busy, but I have found myself wondering how you balance celebrating the interesting idiosyncrasies of these amazing individuals with whom we work with helping them "fit in" or at least not be avoided. I currently have an eighth grader who can tell you that when she sings to herself (gestures/pointing and all) in the bleachers at recess others have weird thoughts about her, but she wants to do it more than she cares about what others think. She likes the attention. We've talked about other ways to get attention, but so far no change. And I have another student who consistently talks to himself in the hallway. Any thoughts?

Elyse Graves
Speech-Language Pathologist
Beavercreek City Schools

I understand where this colleague is coming from. Where exactly is the line between interesting information and too much information, between interest and obsession? Students with ASD often engage in self-stimulating behaviors when the stimulation they need is not available in the environment, such as repeatedly rubbing or slapping their hands together to gain tactile input (Bright, Bittick, & Fleeman, 1981), or covering their ears to block out loud noises to help decrease or regulate the sensations they are experiencing (Storey, Bates, McGhee, & Dycus, 1984).

If our students need to move or stim to regulate their sensory systems in order to function better, why are we stopping them? Don't we all use certain coping strategies throughout the course of a day? I teach students that these behaviors are not good or bad, but explain that they can be perceived as unusual and can cause others to have negative thoughts about them. Then I help them determine when and where it is appropriate to talk about their special interest or to stim. For example, it's fine to talk to someone about your special interest if you know they are also interested in the topic and if you allow them to make comments and join the conversation; however, it is not okay to bore others to satisfy your need to spew all the information floating in your head. It's fine to stim in the privacy of your own home and some other settings (my classroom at lunch, for example), but you should try to avoid it when you are around mostly neurotypicals who may not understand and may find this behavior unexpected.

Chapters 1 and 2, "Getting Acquainted With Ourselves and Others" and "Self-Awareness," of *Becoming Aware* (Walker, 2013) include information about self-disclosure, loneliness, self-image, perception, personality types, and self-esteem. These topics are rarely covered in the general curriculum, yet they can have a lasting impact on how young adults see themselves and how others perceive them. This kind of information can also help them to see that if there are areas of their life they are not happy about, they can adjust their behavior to gain the desired outcome.

Again, the point is not to change any of these individuals' natural gifts and talents, but to teach self-awareness and then enable them to adjust their behavior based on their environment, audience, and desired outcome. The lessons in this unit are designed to help students know themselves better so they can find personal fulfillment and success.
Lessons in Unit 2 include:

- Personality test

- Music and me project

- Inspiration around us

Survival Skills for the 21st Century Used in This Unit

Critical thinking and problem solving, collaboration across networks and leading by influence, initiative and entrepreneurialism, effective oral and written communication, and curiosity and imagination.

(Opening art) Grace is a senior in PEERspective. She is a triplet and often struggles to feel like she fits in at both school and home. Grace has said that PEERspective gives her the opportunity to increase her confidence and work on her social skills in a safe environment.

Unit 2: Self-Awareness, Self-Acceptance, Disclosure
Lesson 1: Personality Test

Materials

- Internet access (16personalities.com/free-personality-test) and a device such as phone, iPad, computer
- Paper and pens to take notes (one per student; optional)
- Unit 2, Handout 1

Duration

One 50-minute class period with possible follow-up the next school day depending on the discussion depth

Lesson Overview

The students do an on-line assessment to determine their personality type. (It takes 20-40 minutes.) Completing this exercise is difficult for some students because they have to go with their first instinct and not over-analyze each question; furthermore, there are no right or wrong answers. After finishing the assessment, students get their results, which are supposed to reflect their natural tendencies based on their personality type. After everyone has completed the assessment and read about the descriptions attached to their personality type, ask students to raise their hands if they agree with the findings. This can lead to a class discussion about how each of us has strengths and weaknesses based on our personality type.

Student Objectives

1. The students will complete the assessment online.
2. The students will discover their personality type and then read about it.
3. The students will participate in a class discussion on whether or not they agree with the findings of the personality assessment, as well as how we all have strengths and weaknesses due to our personality, and that we are all unique.

Rationale

This lesson is designed to assist the students in realizing that we are all created different and that is a good thing. At the same time, students will discover that many of their classmates have the same or similar personality types. During the discussion, students may also discover that one of their classmates is naturally quiet, but that they had never realized it before because she "forces" herself to make conversation and advocate for her needs. This may, in turn, lead to the realization that they can try to do the same. Personality types are not "good" or "bad." Everybody has strengths and weaknesses based on their natural tendencies.

NPDC Evidence-Based Practices Used in This Lesson

- Cognitive behavioral intervention
- Computer-aided instruction
- Self-management

47

Personality Test

Today you will take an assessment designed to determine your personality type. Pick the first answer that comes to mind and don't over-think each question. Also, be sure that you are honest and take your time when responding.

1. Go to 16personalities.com/free-personality-test or search for "16 personalities."

2. Take the assessment.

3. Record your findings here:_____.

4. Read about your specific personality type and take notes below.

5. Do you agree or disagree with these findings? Why?

6. What are your strengths based on this assessment?

7. What careers are people with your personality type best suited for? Have you thought about choosing any of these careers?

8. What do you think may be some obstacles for people who share your personality type?

9. What other students share your personality type? Are you surprised, why or why not?

10. What are your takeaways from today's lesson?

Unit 2: Self-Awareness, Self-Acceptance, Disclosure
Lesson 2: Music and Me Project

Materials

- Song
- Device for playing the song (computer, CD player, iPod speaker)
- Unit 2, Lesson 2 Handout

Duration

One or two 50-minute class periods, depending on depth of explanation and number of students

Lesson Overview

Each student brings a song to class that is meaningful to them. The song must be school appropriate and pre-approved by the teacher (students can search the name of the song and "clean version" to ensure that the song is school appropriate, if you are unsure, I suggest listening to it prior to class with headphones). The students discuss their song choice in groups of four prior to individually sharing a portion of the song with the class. After the song is played, the student presenting shares why she chose the specific song and what it means to her.

Student Objectives

1. The students will prepare a song that is meaningful to them and share it with the class.
2. The students will share the meaning behind the song.
3. The students will complete Unit 2, Handout 2.

Rationale

This lesson allows the students to share a little about themselves through music and helps them find connections with others based on similar tastes in music. The activity also shows students that everyone has different likes and dislikes, and that the world would be boring if we all liked the exact same things, just as this activity would be boring if everyone chose the same song. (Even if two people choose the same song, chances are that their rationales for choosing it differs from person to person based on their past experiences.) The activity helps the students start disclosing who they are and what has influenced their lives while showing that we all see things through different lenses, influenced by our personal life journey.

NPDC Evidence-Based Practices Used in This Lesson
- Computer-aided instruction
- Developmental relationship-based treatment
- Peer-mediated instruction
- Modeling

Music and Me

Your task is to choose a song to share with your classmates. The song should have a special meaning for you. You must play the song for the class. Be prepared to share your rationale for choosing this particular song after you play it for the class. Also, be sure that if there is any bad language in your song choice that you use only the edited version (please type in "radio-edited version" to ensure the song is school-appropriate).

Song choice:

Rationale:

My takeaways from this lesson:

Other takeaways I found interesting:

Unit 2: Self-Awareness, Self-Acceptance, Disclosure
Lesson 3: Inspiration Around Us

Materials

- *Temple Grandin* (Ferguson & Jackson, 2010) – HBO movie
- DVD player and/or computer with smartboard

Duration

Two or three 50-minute class periods

Lesson Overview

The class watches the HBO film *Temple Grandin* (Ferguson & Jackson, 2010). After viewing the movie and discussing it as a class, the students work in pairs to choose a movie, video clip, book, or article about someone they find inspirational – the person does not have to have autism or any other disability. The pair must select one of the suggested sources within one class period.

Student Objectives

1. The students will work cooperatively to decide on their inspirational source.
2. The students will prepare their rationale and presentation, and present a copy of the source.
3. The students will present the project to the class.
4. The students will discover that many inspiring people have had to overcome things in their lives and they can, too.

Rationale

Teaching students with HFA that their perspective is not the only perspective can be challenging. This lesson is designed to continue to foster rapport through personal topics and working in pairs. Students work together to decide not only what inspires them personally, but also what is meaningful to their partner. The partners team up and decide on their one source, along with their rationale for choosing it. They both present to the class and are both responsible for having the source available to share.

Working collaboratively, compromising, preparation, presenting, and rapport building are all intentional components of this lesson. While the concept of "start to finish" can be effective for students on the spectrum, sometimes they perseverate on the details or the need to be "right." Many students on the spectrum need to have closure when doing assignments and/or class projects and don't handle it well if they don't have a "finish." In addition to meeting a tight timeline, in this activity students practice the skills needed to compromise and see others' points of view. The undertone of the lesson is for students to work around whatever obstacles they encounter in life to become successful and content.

NPDC Evidence-Based Practices Used in This Lesson
• Computer-aided instruction
• Developmental relationship-based treatment

Additional Activities and Ideas for Unit 2

- **Talent Days:** It is amazing how many talents and varying interests students have. Allowing them to show off their unique talents or special interests is a great way to help students get comfortable speaking in front of a class, as part of their widening social skills repertory.

  One of my students, Ben, brought in paper for everybody and taught us origami. Since we were all beginners, he taught us an "easy" bird – but we found it far from easy! The frustration felt in the room slowly dissipated, however, when one of the peer coaches spoke up and asked if Ben would teach us again, but "act like we are kindergarteners this time." Ben slowly went through the steps again, and we all ended up creating our own origami with a somewhat similar likeness to a bird. Ben glowed with pride as his friends thanked him for helping them make their own "easy" origami.

  These types of moments may seem like a distraction from more "important" academic lessons, but they are teaching all of the students more about communication, problem solving, and patience than anything scripted could.

- **Nonverbal Communication:** In order to understand that their behavior is being perceived as unusual or odd and, therefore, a hindrance to successful interactions with others, it is important for students to learn how to pick up on nonverbal communication. Many students miss out on information because they are not able to easily decipher body language. If indeed, as reported (Yaffe, 2011), 93% of our communication is nonverbal, then our students are missing out on a lot of vital information.

  Teachers come to me, frustrated that a student with HFA did not react to their "teacher look" in class. Again, "why didn't they just say that?" is the usual response I get when I discuss this with the student who got in trouble because of what appeared to be rude and defiant behavior. Like rapport building, teaching nonverbal communication should be a consistent theme throughout PEERspective.

- **Overcoming Obstacles:** Consider having a guest speaker who has overcome an obstacle in his or her life and found success. This could be a precursor or wrapup for Unit 2, Lesson 4. Over the years, I have become friends with some amazing people on the spectrum. One close friend is Sean Barron, a successful author and speaker. Sean is in a healthy relationship, works at a local newspaper, and he continues to write books on various subjects. Sean has adopted my PEERspective students as his "God Children." While you may not have contact with a well-known person with autism like Sean, there are many other success stories available to choose from. The point is to show, through the lives of others, that although autism and other disabilities can pose struggles in one's life, it can also be a gift.

- **Ted Talks:** If you are not able to find a guest speaker on your own, an alternative would be to show a Ted Talk (https://www.ted.com/talks). This resource gives you and your students access to a multitude of inspirational stories and examples of success.

- **Quote Wall:** My students' insights continue to amaze me. Over the years, I have jotted down student quotes on sticky notes and put them on my classroom wall. This is a way to celebrate our different ways of thinking. It can also be a way to explain sarcasm or social nuances otherwise overlooked. For example, if a quote is added to the board and a student on the spectrum doesn't understand why other people in the class found it funny, that is a great teachable moment to explain the "why." These teachable moments are invaluable and the quote stays on the board the whole year so it's a constant reminder of the lesson that was learned. Towards the end of the year, the students on the spectrum will laugh and recognize that a quote is sarcastic.

  At the end of the year, the students work together to create a quote poster that is displayed in my classroom for years to come. (All of the titles for the chapters in this book are from my quote wall.) So when former students come to visit me after they graduate, the first thing they look for is their class's quote poster.

- **Johari Window:** The Johari Window (Luft, 1969) is a model that describes the relationship between self-disclosure and self-awareness. Chapters 1 and 2 of *Becoming Aware* (Walker, 2013) and the lesson plan supplement include lessons about how we all have areas that we hide from ourselves and others. This concept can help students on the spectrum in multiple ways. Learning that they don't have to tell everything in order to be an honest person and that everyone keeps certain areas hidden can be a powerful revelation.

- **Self-Change Project:** A supplemental lesson from Chapter 2 of *Becoming Aware* (Walker, 2013) is the self-change project. This can be a little tricky, so you need to be sure that your students are able to decipher the difference between wanting to change something about oneself and "reinventing" oneself. It's important that students understand that we are not trying to change who they are, but that we all have areas of our lives that we would like to change and improve upon.

One day a few years ago while taking attendance, I noticed that one of my students (Levi) was missing. I had seen him earlier in the day, he wasn't on the early dismissal list, and he was not one to skip class, so I got a little nervous. When I asked the other students in the class if they had seen him, one of them looked at me very confused and said that he had just seen Levi, who had told him something about working on his self-change project. Upon some investigation, we found Levi in the weight room "pumping iron." His self-change project was to get fit and gain muscle, so naturally he was working on that during PEERspective! Levi continues to work out with a trainer several days a week, and is by now a very fit young man. Besides, the consistent exercise has helped his anxiety and increased his self-esteem.

- **Wacky Wednesday:** Helping students become more aware of their surroundings is important. Indeed, being aware of one's surroundings is a part of not only becoming more socially aware, but can also be important for safety.

  I have taught this often neglected area by choosing a student to dress or act "wacky" to exhibit unexpected behavior (e.g., having a student wear his shirt inside out or having a student answer everything with a "yes" or "no"). I usually do it just once a month, on a Wednesday. This gives students a clue about when it will happen without making it too obvious. The point is for the students to recognize that something is a little different and then to acknowledge that difference. I prompt the peer coaches not to "play" or guess, so that the target students can discover what is "off."

UNIT 3:
Relationships

"I just realized that the world doesn't revolve around me." – Sam

At first glance, the above quote may seem pretty obvious. The funny thing is that many students on the autism spectrum don't naturally realize that other people have valid thoughts and feelings, too. One day in class, a student, Sam, announced loudly that he realized that the world didn't revolve around him. He was not joking, nor is he a spoiled kid; but he was still discovering the importance of social awareness and perspective taking. Luckily, those things can be taught, and should be, because they will have a lasting impact. Sam, like many others on the spectrum, is both thoughtful and kind, but this didn't shine through until he learned that he needed to be more aware of the people around him.

Often, students on the autism spectrum, like Sam, don't realize that their thoughts and feelings are not the only thoughts and feelings in the world (Loveland & Tunali-Kotoski, 2005). It is understandable then, that these individuals often struggle with relationships. While you could argue that one can go through life without a romantic relationship or friendships, one thing is sure: Relationships matter in the workforce! While I hope that my students will enjoy many social relationships in their lives, I know it is imperative that they are able to communicate with others and form relationships in order to be successful members of society. According to Dale Carnegie's well-known book, *How to Win Friends and Influence People*, while "15% of one's financial success is due to one's technical knowledge, about 85% is due to skill in human engineering to personality and the ability to lead people" (Carnegie, 1981, p. xvi). In other words, people lose their jobs because they don't have good people skills, not because they are incompetent.

Chapter 6, "Developing Close Relationships," of *Becoming Aware* (Walker, 2013) is the perfect tool for discussions about things ranging from how friendships start all the way to how to develop romantic relationships. Given that the thinking of students with ASD tends to be "black and white" (Grandin, 2010), these subjects can be challenging.

For example, when talking about their plans for future personal relationships, students usually give a range of responses, varying from "No way am I ever getting married" to "I'm going to be married with one child by the time I am 30." Whether these are valid options for a given student or not, teaching about developing solid relationships and understanding the perspective of others can help students achieve whatever goal they might have, and, more important, build relationships that will help them be successful in the workplace.

Peer coaches are vital tools in helping students with ASD understand and develop personal relationships, as illustrated in the following example.

An amazing student, Ben, had made an intricate origami creation to give to a girl in his band class, but he was not sure if it was a good way to get her to notice him. His friend, who is a coach, explained that it would be best to have some conversations with her first, and then possibly give her the origami if the opportunity arose. Though Ben agreed that this was the best solution, after several days when we asked him if he had spoken to the girl yet, he reported that he had not.

Colby, the coach, jumped up and asked a student in the group, Mary, to play the role of "band girl" and proceeded to act out a conversation about one of the small talk topics we had discussed earlier that week in class (see Unit 3, Handout 6). He asked Mary, acting as "band girl," if she thought the snow storm that was predicted would help us to have a snow day, and with that the conversation was off and running! Then, Ben practiced starting a conversation.

Not only did Colby help stop a potentially devastating social situation for Ben, he also coached his friend on how to start a conversation and how to ease into letting a girl know you like her. Without a firm foundation of friendship and trust, Ben would not have brought up his plan to gift "band girl" with the origami, and he certainly would not have accepted social coaching from Colby through role-play. Through developing rapport and friendships with peer coaches, students learn how to develop social relationships that will help them throughout their lives.

Kaylee and Josh, partners on the mock date, which is a part of the spring field trip.

Lessons in Unit 3 include:

- Experts for a day

- Relationship Interviews

- Letter to my future companion

- Film study

Survival Skills for the 21st Century Used in This Unit

Critical thinking and problem solving, collaboration across networks and leading by influence, agility and adaptability, initiative and entrepreneurialism, effective oral and written communication, accessing and analyzing information, and curiosity and imagination.

(Opening art) Ben is the student artist for this chapter. I met Ben when my oldest daughter, Elyse, was in middle school. She and Ben's sister were in show choir together. One day, I had to take Elyse to their house so his mom, Meredith, could measure her for her costume. At that time, Ben hibernated in the basement and didn't make eye contact. Today, he is planning to go to college and has been a member of our high school band for all four years. When asked for her advice for raising a child with autism, Meredith said with tears in her eyes, "Build on their strengths and never give up." Sounds like good advice for any parent.

Unit 3: Relationships
Lesson 1: Experts for a Day

Materials

- *Becoming Aware*, Chapter 6, "Developing Close Relationships" (Walker, 2013)
- Unit 3, Handout 1
- Paper/pen/markers/crayons for each group
- Assignment explanation sheet and rubric, Unit 3, Handout 1

Duration

Five 50-minute class periods, three for project work days and at least two for presentations

Lesson Overview

The students work in small groups to create a lesson plan and present their lesson based upon an assigned section of Chapter 6, "Developing Close Relationships," of *Becoming Aware* (Walker, 2013). They have three days in class to complete the required components in their groups. The students will then present the lesson during their assigned class period, thus becoming the "Experts for a Day."

Student Objectives

1. The students will practice skills needed to productively work in a group, including compromise, delegating, listening to others' opinions, and communicating their ideas in a socially acceptable way.

2. The students will work effectively in groups to create their lesson.

3. The students will read and discuss content about relationships.

Rationale

Group work is an essential part of life. Not being able to get along with others prevents people in the workforce from reaching their potential and greatly impacts relationships outside of work. This lesson is designed to allow students to practice working in a group through an authentic project. Students take turns being the team leader throughout the school year; this enables them to practice being in charge, but doing so in an appropriate way. The students have an incentive to work together because they will need to be experts in order to present the project to the class. Using Chapter 6 of *Becoming Aware*, about relationships, is an intentional way to get the students to talk about a personal topic.

NPDC Evidence-Based Practices Used in This Lesson

- Computer-aided instruction
- Developmental relationship-based treatment
- Peer-mediated instruction
- Modeling

Experts for a Day

Guess what? You are now the experts! Work as a group to plan and then teach pages_____ in *Becoming Aware*. You must work together when designing your lesson; be sure that your lesson includes:

1. A journal prompt based on the topic of your section, designed for peer response

2. One visual aid (poster, PowerPoint, etc.)

3. One activity (a game, survey, etc.)

The team leader that your group has chosen has the final say, but all group members must voice their opinions. On the presentation day, everyone MUST have a role that includes speaking. You will be graded on how well you work in a group. In addition to points for in class work, you will be graded on the attached rubric. This assignment is worth 100 points, but even more important is that working in a group and listening to others' opinions is a lifelong skill you need to be successful in life.

BRAINSTORMING:

Notes/Ideas:

Journal Prompt …

Visual Aid Ideas …

Rubric for Experts for a Day						
Student(s) Name:						
Assignment: *Experts for a Day*				**Date Completed:**		
	Excellent	**Good**	**Average**	**Needs Improvement**	**Total Points Possible**	**Rating**
Criteria 1 – Creativity: Added creative insights or twists to the chosen lesson.	18-20	14-18	8-14	>8	20	
Criteria 2 – Knowledge: Demonstrated an understanding of the information and chose the most important topics.	16-18	12-16	8-12	>8	18	
Criteria 3 – Craftsmanship: Neat, clean, and complete.	16-18	12-16	8-12	>8	18	
Criteria 4 – Effort: Took time to develop ideas and complete the lesson, Project finished ON TIME.	18-20	14-18	8-14	>8	20	
Criteria 5 – Met All Requirements: Journal, visual aid, activity, shared information.	10-12	8-10	5-8	>5	12	
Criteria 6 – Presentation: The presenters were organized, prepared, and enthusiastic. Everyone participated.	10-12	8-10	5-8	>5	12	

Unit 3: Relationships
Lesson 2: Relationship Interview

Materials

- Unit 3, Handout 3
- Student journals
- Pens/pencil and paper or computer for word processing

Duration

Two 50-minute class periods and time at home for the interview

Lesson Overview

The students interview someone who is in a relationship that they feel is healthy or ideal, based on class discussions and personal perspective. This can be a romantic relationship or a friendship. Each student receives a list of five questions that they can use in their interview, but they have to write five additional questions on their own (for a total of 10). The students record the answers to the 10 questions and then reflect on the interview with a follow-up journal entry. Finally, they discuss their findings in class and compile five takeaways from the interviews that they feel has the biggest impact on healthy relationships.

Student Objectives

1. The students will choose someone to interview based on their observations of what a healthy relationship looks like. They can choose a parent, sibling, neighbor, or friend.

2. The students will receive five prepared questions, write five interview questions of their own before the interview, and record the answers to all questions. They will also answer the journal prompt prior to the class discussion.

3. The students will share their findings throughout the whole class discussion and contribute to the list on the board of possible takeaways.

Rationale

To complete this activity, the students apply several of the skills they have been working on. First, they need to think about what is important in a relationship. The questions already written for them will allow them to have a framework and examples for when they write their interview questions. They also need to ask someone if they can interview them, as well as explain the reason for the interview. These communication skills will be utilized throughout the interview process. The post-interview journal entry will encourage students to reflect on what they can take away from this project. Finally, the students will each share and contribute to the class discussion and compilation of common threads. In order to come up with only five common threads, the students will need to listen to others' opinions and mostly like have to compromise.

> **NPDC Evidence-Based Practices Used in This Lesson**
> - Cognitive behavioral intervention
> - Computer-aided instruction
> - Developmental relationship-based treatment
> - Scripting

Relationship Interview

Name_____ Date_____

1. Who are you currently in a relationship with and how long have you been in this relationship?

2. What do you like about the person you are in a relationship with? Why are these things important to you?

3. How much time do you spend with this person in the course of a week?

4. What struggles do you have in this relationship? How do you overcome these obstacles?

5. What do you feel is the most important part of having a successful relationship?

Please record your five interview questions and answer the journal prompt below after you have completed the interview.

Journal: After completing this interview, what are five takeaways? What do you feel is the most important aspect of a healthy relationship and why?

Unit 3: Relationships
Lesson 4: Letter to My Future Companion

Materials

- Unit 3, Handouts 4 & 5
- Pens/pencils and paper or computer for word processing

Duration

Three 50-minute class periods

Lesson Overview

The students write a letter to their future companion. After reviewing the assignment (see Unit 3, Handout 4) and brainstorming possible criteria as a class, the students are given time to write/ type their letters. The students present their letter to the class, including the specified number of criteria.

Student Objectives

1. The students will consider what criteria are important to them with regard to a future romantic relationship. These criteria are often similar to what they are looking for in a friend.
2. The students will compose, type, and submit a letter that meets the established criteria from the given rubric.
3. The students will present their work to the class.

Rationale

This assignment reinforces writing skills being taught in language arts classes. In addition, students will have to decide what personality traits and overall criteria are most important to them when considering potential relationships. A critical part of this is the recognition that they are valuable and worthy of being selective about whom they decide to spend their time with. They also need to understand that while these are the ideal criteria they are looking for, they need to be open to the fact that no person is perfect and that often not all of their criteria will be met.

> **NPDC Evidence-Based Practices Used in This Lesson**
> - Cognitive behavioral intervention
> - Computer-aided instruction
> - Developmental relationship-based treatment

Letter to My Future Companion

- Write a letter to your future companion. In this letter, you must include five criteria that are important to you (for example, sense of humor, same religion, nice-looking, kind-hearted). These criteria often change and shift over time, so just use the criteria that are important to you now. Keep in mind that while these are your current ideal criteria, you may or may not find someone who meets all of them – and that's okay.

- Write the letter in a friendly, informal letter format, and use your time wisely in class in order to meet the assignment deadline. Finally, be sure to include one quote that expresses how you feel about love. You will present this letter to the class, but you will only share what you are comfortable sharing.

- Please see the rubric for a breakdown of point values so you know how you will be graded.

- Many students have said that this assignment really helped them to decide what to look for in a boyfriend/girlfriend. As you decide what is most important to you, think back over what we learned in Chapter 6 of *Becoming Aware*.

Assessment Rubric for Letter to Future Companion						
Student(s) Name:					**Class Period:**	
Assessment of Learning					**Date Completed:**	
	Excellent	**Good**	**Average**	**Needs Improvement**	**Total Points Possible**	**Teacher's Rating**
Criteria 1: Used at least five criteria with detailed explanations.	18-20	14-18	8-14	>8	20	
Criteria 2: Used the class time effectively and took the assignment seriously.	18-20	14-18	8-14	>8	20	
Criteria 3: Used a friendly letter format; good grammar, spelling, and overall flow.	9-10	7-8	6-5	>5	10	
Criteria 4 : Included a quote about love/ relationships that defines how the writer feels and explained what it means to him/her.	9-10	7-8	6-5	>5	10	

Final Grade =   /60

Presentation Points =   /20

Comments:

Unit 3: Relationships
Lesson 5: Film Study

Materials

- Unit 3, Handouts 6 and 7
- Student journals
- Pens/pencils and paper or computer for word processing

Duration

One 50-minute class period

Lesson Overview

The students watch video clips that deal with relationships. After each clip, the students individually write down some "dos" and "don'ts" based on the clip that they viewed. Recommendations include clips from are such movies as *How to Lose a Guy in 10 Days* (Petrie, 2003) and *Hitch* (Lassiter, Smith, Zee, & Tennant, 2005).

For example, I had a student who tended to come on too strong when he liked someone and called/texted too often. I showed the clip from *How to Lose a Guy in 10 Days* where the character of Andi incessantly contacts Ben, which really annoys him. Another option is the sitcom *Big Bang Theory*. Many clips from this show work for this unit, but the one I usually use is the episode that shows the flow chart that Sheldon designed with a Friendship Algorithm.

I have found that using YouTube when showing clips is the easiest way to ensure that you don't waste class time on parts that don't pertain to what you are teaching and that you exclude anything that would not be classroom appropriate.

Student Objectives:

1. The students will watch each video clip and think about what is going well with communication in the relationship and what isn't.

2. The students will record several "dos" and "don'ts" in their journals.

3. The students will share their findings throughout the whole class discussion.

Rationale

Using video clips allows you to take the personal nature out of navigating relationships. It also helps create a common experience to discuss – some students have had relationships and others have not. Finally, it is much easier to pick out the mistakes others are making than our own. If we can start to recognize these things in others, then we will be more aware of our own actions and how they might be perceived.

NPDC Evidence-Based Practices Used in This Lesson

- Cognitive behavioral intervention
- Computer-aided instruction
- Developmental relationship-based treatment
- Peer-mediated instruction and intervention
- Self-management
- Video modeling

Small Talk

You will be working in groups of two or three to create conversation cards. Conversation cards are small cards that have conversation starters and/or questions written on them. Small talk is very important and can change based on the situation and the participants. For example, small talk with a friend or peer is very different from small talk with a boss or teacher. Each group will present their cards and then we will use the cards to simulate different situations.

_____ list 20 topics to discuss (100 pts)

_____ put on the template provided, laminate, cut, and put on a ring (15 pts)

_____ add a cover card with the topic and your names and a blank back card (10 pts)

_____ creativity (use of color, graphics, border) (15 pts)

_____ /140 points possible

Notes/Brainstorming:

Conversation Card Templates

Other Activities and Ideas for Unit 3

- **Debate:** The age-old question "Can men and women be just friends?" is a great debate topic for this unit. Debates are a natural way to help the students learn to see others' perspectives. You can decide which point of view each student will take or you can allow students to choose (assuming the two points of view are close to equally divided). This activity helps students learn to accept differing opinions and the grey area of not having a "winning" side. Because there is no definitive "winner," this activity can be challenging for students on the spectrum, but if you continue to do them throughout the year, it becomes much easier.

- **Guest Speaker(s):** Several groups would be appropriate to contact to obtain names of possible guest speakers. In our area the group that I have used is called Marriage Works (trustmarriage.com). This is an organization that is designed to help people have strong marriages through counseling and workshops. A counselor, therapist, or psychologist would also be good options. The foundation of a healthy relationship is communication, so this activity could be implemented at any point during the school year.

- **Cartooning:** Provide students with two cartoon strip templates. One of the strips could be a scenario of something that shouldn't be done in relationships (e.g., being too needy), and the other strip could demonstrate something that important to do (e.g., communicate your feelings). Many students are artistically talented, and this type of lesson allows them to show that!

- **Game:** The board game *Battle of the Sexes* (Spin Master; https://www.spinmaster.com) is fun to play. But be sure to go through the cards and take out any that are not school appropriate.

- **Role-Play:** Role-play is essential for this unit, including such aspects of relationships as asking someone out, meeting your date's parents, small talk with someone you like, discussing something that is bothering you in a relationship, etc. You can record the role-plays to critique right after, or even later in the year. It is interesting to record role-plays at the beginning of the year, half way, and then at the end of the year. The students enjoy seeing the progress both in themselves and in their peers. Watching the videos is a form of video modeling (Wilson, 2013); it allows the students to see how they communicate, critique themselves, and then make changes as needed.

UNIT 4:
Managing Stress and Wellness

"If you're trampled and killed on Black Friday, I will avenge your death." – Nick S.

When Nick came into my room in a panic after school the day before Thanksgiving break, I knew immediately that something was wrong. After all, this wasn't his regular end-of-the day routine. He proceeded to tell me that if I was killed over break, he would avenge my death. He then quickly turned around and left. I was puzzled for a minute, but then remembered sharing with the class that my Mom and I had a tradition of shopping on the day after Thanksgiving each year. I guess you would be worried about someone's well-being if all you knew of Black Friday was what you had seen on the news.

Life can be stressful! Stress management is a vital part not only of living a long, healthy life, but also for overall quality of life. We all have times when we need to de-escalate. In addition to the toll stress can take on our emotional and physical health, if we don't learn to calm ourselves, we will communicate less effectively. That is, when anger is our reaction to stress, for example, we may cause lose our temper and say and do things that we will later regret and that have a negative impact on others around us.

People on the spectrum have a difficult time with emotion recognition and regulation (Geller, 2005), which can lead to difficulties in future relationships and overall health and well-being. Therefore, it is important for them to learn to self-regulate to an even greater extent.

The lessons in this unit not only illustrate the negative effects of stress on our lives, but also show the benefits of positive stress. Chapter 8, "Managing Stress and Wellness," of *Becoming Aware* (Walker, 2013) is a great tool to use when teaching about stress management and the different types of stress. Sometimes we forget that some stress is not only okay, but can actually be good for you. Eustress refers to good, or short-term, stress that strengthens us for immediate physical activity, creativity, and enthusiasm (Walker, 2013). Helping students realize that stress isn't "black or white" or "good or bad" can enable them to deal with it in a healthier way.

Along with learning the different types of stress and the effects stress has on our bodies, we try out different types of stress-relieving techniques. For example, a zumba instructor comes to the school to teach a zumba fitness class. While at first glance this looks like we are just trying to teach the students how doing cardiovascular exercise can reduce stress (APA, 2016), in reality, it is so much more.

Zumba is a type of cardio-respiratory exercise that most teens on the spectrum have not tried, so trying it pushes them outside of their comfort zone. As discussed in an earlier chapter, when we push ourselves outside our comfort zone, we can set ourselves up to gain social success (Merrell & Gimpel, 1998; Myles, Aspy, Mataya, & Shaffer, 2017). This activity is also a shared experience, which helps build friendships, and, finally, frankly, it's fun. Laughter has been a proven way to reduce stress (Smith & Segal, 2016); and this activity definitely lends itself to lots of laughter. Teaching students not to take themselves so seriously is a lesson in and of itself, especially with this population.

Over the past few years, this unit has fallen right at semester exam time, which has prompted me to create a "sampler" session of stress-reducing activities. We do 20 minutes of zumba, 20 minutes of yoga, and about 10 minutes of relaxation, meditation, and visualization. Then the students type up a stress-management plan based on what has worked for them in the past as well as the new strategies (zumba, yoga, visualization) they have tried recently. This can be done as a larger lesson or exam, as I use it, or the lesson can be done over several days. Either way, it is a fun way to continue to build relationships and shared experiences, which naturally continue the rapport building that we started on day one.

Learning how to effectively work through stressful situations is an important life skill. Virginia Satir, an American author and social worker referenced in *Becoming Aware* (Walker, 2013), reminds us that "Life is not what it's supposed to be. It's what it is. The way you cope with it is what makes the difference" (p. 356). These lifelong coping skills could be one of the most important and life-changing things you can teach your students.

NPDC Evidence-Based Practices Used in This Lesson

- Computer-aided instruction
- Exercise
- Imitation-based interaction

Lessons in Unit 4 include:

- Stress management midterm
- In the media
- Mantras

Survival Skills for the 21st Century Used in Unit

Agility and adaptability, effective oral and written communication, accessing and analyzing information, and curiosity and imagination.

(Opening art) Lexie is a peer coach in PEERspective. She is very artistic and expresses herself through her photography and her unconventional make-up. Talented, fun students like Lexie helps make the class interesting and fun.

Unit 4: Managing Stress and Wellness
Lesson 1: Stress Management Midterm

Unit 4, Handout 1

Stress Management Reflection/Midterm Exam

Step 1 – Introduction

Discuss how you have dealt with stress in the past and how it impacted your life.

1-paragraph response (written or typed)

Step 2 – Identify the Stressors in Your Life

Think about what is causing stress in your life and determine possible reasons why.

1-paragraph response

Step 3 – Identify the Top Five Ways You Will Fight the Above Stressors

5-paragraph response – remember to talk about why you think each strategy will benefit you and consider using some of the stress reducers we tried today or talked about in class.

Stress Management Rubric

Name:_____Period_____

Practical:

_____ /10: Dressed appropriately (tennis shoes and workout clothing)

_____ /10: Good attitude

_____ /40: Student was engaged and participated throughout the exam

_____ /60

Comments:

Written:

Stress Management Plan

_____ /10 outlined plan using at least five techniques

_____ /10 detailed explanation of rationale behind techniques

_____ / 10 met length requirement, typed

_____ /5 used time wisely

_____ /40

Comments:

Total Score_____/100

Midterm Evaluation

Answer the following questions. Please be honest and really think about your answer to each.

1. What has been the most difficult thing about being in PEERspective so far this year?

2. What has been the most engaging activity we have done so far, and how has it helped you personally?

3. What has been the most helpful topic we have covered and how have you applied it to your life?

4. What would you say is the least effective activity we have done?

5. How have used your communication skills in class this year?

6. How do you feel about our drama lessons (role-play Wednesday, etc.)?

7. What did you like/dislike about our field trips?

8. What improvements have you seen in your communication skills since being in PEERspective?

9. What else do you feel you need to work on to effectively communicate daily?

10. Overall, how was first semester? How are your classes and your interaction with your peers, both in class and at lunch? How does this compare to last year?

11. What else can your teacher(s) do to help you? What suggestions do you have?

12. What social/communication goal do you have for yourself before the end of this school year?

Unit 4: Managing Stress and Wellness
Lesson 2: In the Media

Materials

- Four current articles on stress
- Unit 4, Handout 4
- Student journals
- Papers/pens (one per student)

Duration

One 50-minute period

Lesson Overview

Many health and fitness magazines and/or online sources contain articles on the effects of stress and how to manage stress. In this lesson, the students read an article and then journal about and/or discuss it. This can be done in a variety of ways, but I like to use something I call "Four Corners." The students are divided in groups of four, and each group reads, discusses, and takes notes on one article. Then the group members are mixed up, and each new group of four shares with the other groups about the article they read and discussed. This activity allows you to cover a lot of material in a short time, and also requires students to share and teach about their original article.

Student Objectives

1. The students will read an article individually and then discuss it with their small group.

2. The students will collectively decide on the most important aspects of the original article and prepare to share with their next group.

3. The students will share the information with their second group and take notes on information shared with them by their peers (this is the process for all three groups).

Rationale

This lesson helps students obtain current information about stress. The students in each group gain information from three other sources by the end of the lesson because each group shares the information they learned in their first group to their peers in the other groups, communicating with clarity and conciseness while also answering questions about their article. When engaging in this activity, students decide what the most important parts of their article are, then share their opinion, and listen to others' ideas and perspectives.

NPDC Evidence-Based Practices Used in This Lesson

- Cognitive behavioral intervention
- Imitation-based interaction
- Peer-mediated instruction and intervention
- Self-management
- Modeling

Unit 4: Managing Stress and Wellness
Lesson 3: Mantras

Materials

- Unit 4, Handout 4
- Four current articles on stress
- Student journals
- Papers/pens (one per student)
- *Becoming Aware*, Chapter 8, "Managing Stress and Wellness" (Walker, 2013)

Duration

One 50-minute period

Lesson Overview

Chapter 8, "Managing Stress and Wellness," in *Becoming Aware* (Walker, 2013) discusses irrational and rational beliefs and self-talk. Self-talk is what we say to ourselves about an event or situation. Using the text as a guide, students learn the definitions of related terms and then journal about their experiences with self-talk (either positive or negative). For example: "Words have power. Discuss a time when the dialogue in your head had an impact on your performance in a positive or negative way." After the students have had time to respond to the journal prompt, they share their experiences in a whole-class discussion. Finally, students create their personal mantras. These mantras can be used as a quick "go-to" for positive self-talk throughout the year and beyond. For example, when I am doing something for the first time and I'm nervous, I often tell myself, "Fake it til' you make it," a mantra a friend of mine encouraged me to use when I ran my first half marathon. Mantras, and positive self-talk in general, are powerful tools for success.

Student Objectives

1. The students will learn the definitions of irrational and rational self-talk.

2. The students will reflect on their experience with self-talk through a journal prompt.

3. The students will create their own mantra.

Rationale

This lesson is designed to teach students that what they say to themselves can impact their performance, confidence, and overall outcome in any given situation. As a result, learning to tell themselves positive things can have a positive impact on their lives. Many students on the spectrum struggle with social anxiety, bullying, and failed social interactions, so putting themselves out into the social world is difficult for them. This activity gives students a tool to use when their confidence and overall optimism are wavering.

NPDC Evidence-Based Practices Used in This Lesson

- Cognitive behavioral intervention
- Computer-aided instruction
- Developmental relationship-based treatment
- Self-management

Personal Mantras

Mantra: An expression or idea that is repeated often, usually without thinking about it.

Affirmation: A positive statement or declaration of the truth or existence of something.

Directions: Create your personal mantra, and write it in the space provided below. Be sure your mantra is an affirmation that inspires you. Words matter, so use care when creating your mantra. Then, use this mantra by repeating it to yourself, either in your head or out loud, in situations when you feel less than confident.

Tell yourself something positive today!

Other Ideas and Activities for Unit 4

- **Healthy Living:** Invite a registered dietician to speak to your class about how having a healthy diet can aid in stress management.

- **Stress Management:** Invite someone with post-traumatic stress disorder (PTSD) to speak about his or her experiences dealing with this condition.

- **Motivational Speaker:** Ask a motivational speaker or counselor to come and discuss how attitude and self-talk affects how we deal with stress. (Find someone with a "don't sweat the small stuff" type of mentality.)

- **Self-Assessment:** Review the assessment tools at the end of Chapter 8, "Managing Stress and Wellness," in *Becoming Aware* (Walker, 2013) and consider using them for journaling, discussions, or just as self-awareness. It's helpful to know what stresses one has and how one deals with them before trying to create a new plan of action.

- **Raising Awareness:** Take time to teach about the different types of stress. Use Chapter 8, "Managing Stress and Wellness," in *Becoming Aware* (Walker, 2013) to guide you.

- **Role-Play:** Drama can be a good tool to illustrate what to do and what not to do when dealing with a challenging situation. Break the class into small groups and assign them a stressful scenario. Have each group act out two different ways to deal with the scenario. If the group chooses (or you assign) to act out a negative way to deal with stress, be sure it is followed up with a correct response.

- **Video Modeling:** Consider recording the drama skits and showing them later. As stated in previous chapters, video modeling is an EBP.

UNIT 5:
Conflict Resolution

"There's a world outside my basement?" – Sam

A student in PEERspective, Sam, is a very smart young man who has HFA. The day that he asked if there was a world outside his basement, the students laughed because they knew he was making a joke, but behind this tongue-in-cheek comment was some truth. Sam had confided in me previously that he felt was safer to just hang out alone than having to deal with people. He had been made fun of in the past and had struggled with maintaining relationships. Unfortunately, this isn't an unusual experience for students on the spectrum.

Sam, like many of my students, chose to stay hidden from the world as much as possible, which led a lack of self-esteem and depression. He knew he had to push himself to try social things and learn to develop relationships in order to create the type of future he desired.

All relationships encounter conflict at times, but not all conflict is bad. This concept can be difficult for students on the spectrum to grasp. Due to the often literal/black-and-white thinking of people on the spectrum, conflict can be a difficult thing to overcome. For example, some students assume that if they disagree with someone their relationship with that person is over, not failing to understand that it is okay to disagree or argue, as long as at the end, both parties feel heard and can compromise.

No one enjoys conflict, but it's inevitable in life. This unit has been invaluable to many past students – not just the students on the spectrum but also the coaches. Usually, a couple months into the school year, I receive e-mails similar to the one on the following page.

Mrs. Schmidt,

Hey, how are you? I hope you are doing well and the PEERspective classes are great this year. I just wanted to thank you for teaching me about I-messages. Boy, did that ever come in handy. I am playing football in college, and I live with three other football players. Not only do we have classes and practice together, we also live together ... that's a lot of togetherness. Anyway, I have used I-messages to tell them how I feel when they leave their dishes in the sink, watch TV loudly when I'm trying to sleep, and eat my food. It has helped so much. You were right, it takes the emotion out of the conflict and leads to a more peaceful and quick resolution. I hope to see you at the Homecoming football game in a couple weeks, and I can't wait to meet all the new students. Thanks again! – Michael

---

Most adults haven't mastered the art of peaceful conflict resolution, and yet this college freshman is already putting it to use, thanks to the skills he learned during his time as a PEERspective coach. Encountering conflict with others is not a matter of "if," it's a matter of "when," so it is important to equip our young adults with tools to manage conflict, which can help lead to lasting and meaningful relationships.

Lessons in Unit 5 include:

- I-messages

- Conflict resolution

- Is conflict good or bad?

Survival Skills for the 21st Century Used in This Unit

Critical thinking and problem solving, agility and adaptability, initiative and entrepreneurialism, effective oral and written communication, and accessing and analyzing information.

(Opening art) Allison is the student artist for this chapter. She is a fun, quirky student, who always has a smile on her face. In the past, this smile was to mask her anxiety and stress. She has said that PEERspective allowed her to feel safe and accepted, so now when she smiles, it is a genuine smile.

Unit 5: Conflict Resolution
Lesson 1: I-Messages

Materials

- Unit 5, Handouts 1 and 2
- *Becoming Aware*, Chapter 7, "Resolving Interpersonal Conflict" (Walker, 2013)
- Papers/pens (one per student)
- Computer/smartboard (to project videos)

Duration

Two 50-minute periods, one to complete the handouts and start recording, the other to finish recording and present to the class

Lesson Overview

An I-message "is a way of expressing yourself effectively before you become angry and act in a self-defeating way" (Gordon, 2000, p. 310). I-messages must be taught correctly to be effective in order to teach a set formula for resolving conflict without emotion. Begin by writing the four parts of an I-message on the board or creating a short PowerPoint to relay the appropriate information. After learning the four parts of an I-message: (a) an objective, nonjudgmental description of the person's behavior in specific terms, (b) how I feel about this, (c) the concrete effects on me, and (d) a request and invitation to respond (Walker, 2013), students complete Unit 5, Handout 1. After they complete the handout and discuss it, students role-play how to use an I-message when given a scenario (Unit 5, Handout 2). For additional impact, the skits may be recorded for further analysis by students as an example of video modeling.

Student Objectives

1. The students will learn the four parts of an I-message.

2. The students will be able to write an effective I-message.

3. The students will be able to list at least three scenarios where an I-message would be helpful.

4. The students will role-play using I-messages.

Rationale

I-messages can be very beneficial when trying to be assertive in a respectful way. For students with autism, I-messages serve as a very black-and-white way to solve a conflict and, as such, fit their often literal, black-and-white thinking. More than that, I-messages promote assertiveness. Learning a set structure for being assertive and resolving issues before becoming angry or frustrated is a lifelong skill. By recording the skits, students can see themselves properly conveying I-messages. I have found video modeling to be a very effective teaching tool. If students can see themselves doing something the correct way, they can then recreate the event correctly (Apple et al., 2005; Bellini & Akullian, 2007).

NPDC Evidence-Based Practices Used in This Lesson	
• Cognitive behavioral intervention	• Scripting
• Imitation-based interaction	• Self-management
• Peer-mediated instruction and intervention	• Video modeling

I-Messages

Name_____ Date_____

I-messages (Gordon, 2000) are a way of expressing yourself effectively before you become angry and act in self-defeating ways.

In the space provided below, please take notes about the four parts that make up an I-message (page 310, *Becoming Aware*).

Part 1:

Part 2:

Part 3:

Part 4:

On the back of the handout, write your own I-messages to the following scenarios using the formula suggested.

1. **Scenario:** Your sibling keeps taking your things without asking. Write an I-message to solve this conflict. When you …, I feel … because … Next time …

2. **Scenario:** Your parents keep taking your phone and checking your texts and e-mails when you are not around. They say that it's their right because they pay the bill.
   When you …, I feel … because … Next time …

Act out the following scenario using an I-message. Be sure to include all four parts.

Your friend wants to date your ex-boyfriend/girlfriend that you still have feelings for.

Your parents let your older siblings use the car more than you, even when you ask first.

Your boss isn't giving you the days off that you have requested in advance.

Your parents want you to attend their alma mater, but you would rather attend a different college.

Free choice

Free choice

Unit 5: Conflict Resolution
Lesson 2: Who's in Control?

Materials

- Pencil/pen for each student
- Student journals
- Computer/board/smartboard

Duration

One 50-minute period

Lesson Overview

The students learn that it is important to pick and choose situations when they assert themselves. Students start by responding to a journal prompt: "Name three things that frustrate you that you can control and three things that you can't control." Then, discuss the anonymous quote, "A smart person knows what to say, but a wise person knows whether to say it or not." List 20 scenarios without asking the students which category they fit in. After they are all listed, move them to the appropriate box: Can/Can't Control. Finish with journaling based on the prompt above and/or a discussion about how the lesson relates to conflict resolution.

Student Objectives

1. The students will complete a journal prompt.

2. The students will share their journals with the class.

3. The students will participate in identifying what types of things we can/cannot control based on the teacher's list.

4. The students will discuss or journal about the connection between things we can/cannot control and conflict resolution.

Rationale

While being assertive is an important part of healthy relationships, so is the realization that no one and nothing is perfect. Knowing that many of our students are very literal thinkers (Hobson, 2012), it is important to reiterate the point that there are things we can control and others we cannot. Choosing when and with whom to use our newly perfected I-messages may be as important as teaching how to construct them.

NPDC Evidence-Based Practices Used in This Lesson
- Cognitive behavioral intervention
- Developmental relationship-based treatment
- Peer-mediated instruction and intervention

Unit 5: Conflict Resolution
Lesson 3: Is Conflict Good or Bad?

Materials

- Paper/pens/pencils
- Unit 5, Handout 3
- *Becoming Aware*, Chapter 7, "Resolving Interpersonal Conflict" (Walker, 2013)
- Computer/Internet

Duration

One or two 50-minute periods, dependent upon teacher preference and/or length of debate

Lesson Overview

The students are broken into two groups and randomly assigned a position to defend: (a) why conflict is bad or (b) why conflict is good. Students have 15 minutes to research in their text or on the Internet, take notes, and get prepared for the debate. With the remaining time, allow the students to debate about conflict. Conclude the lesson with a discussion of takeaways about conflict.

Student Objectives

1. The students will work in groups to research and determine the main arguments that support their assigned "view."

2. The students will take turns presenting their arguments.

3. The students will always remain respectful of the other team.

4. The students will take turns, waiting until it is the appropriate time to share their arguments.

5. The students will work as a team, ensuring that all team members speak throughout the time allotted.

Rationale

Perspective taking, or TOM (Baron-Cohen et al., 2013), is one of the most difficult, yet essential, lessons taught in PEERspective. Teaching students to see the other person's point of view is the foundation for teaching them how to think socially. That is, if we cannot see someone else's perspective, we cannot adjust our behavior or dialogue to reach the desired results – whether in our daily interaction with family, friends, and neighbors, or in the workforce where collaboration is a part of most jobs.

If students only see things from their own point of view, they will approach things with a narrow scope of reasoning and problem solving. They may also fixate on having things done their way instead of collaborating for a better result. This specific debate topic is also a great transition to a discussion about why conflict can be both good and bad, depending on how it is handled.

NPDC Evidence-Based Practices Used in This Lesson

- Peer-mediated instruction and intervention
- Self-management

Assessment Rubric						
Student(s) Name:					**Class Period:**	
Assignment: *Debate*					**Date Completed:**	
	Excellent	**Good**	**Average**	**Needs Improvement**	**Total Points Possible**	**Rating**
Criteria 1 – *Group Work*: Each group member was engaged in all aspects of the debate.	18-20	14-18	8-14	>8	20	
Criteria 2 – *Preparation*: The group was prepared, organized, and collected plenty of information supporting their assigned "view."	16-18	12-16	8-12	>8	18	
Criteria 3 – *Presentation*: Each group member did their very best when presenting their view. Voice volume, eye contact, voice inflection/expression, respect of others' opinions and/or statements.	16-18	12-16	8-12	>8	18	
Criteria 4 – *Attitude*: Each group member accepted their assigned "view" and contributed to their group without hesitation or argument.	18-20	14-18	8-14	>8	20	
Criteria 5 – *Debate Rules*: The group followed the structure of the debate.	10-12	8-10	5-8	>5	12	

/100

NOTES:

From Schmidt, J. Why didn't they just say that? Teaching secondary students with high-functioning autism to decode the social world using PEERspective. ©2018 Jennifer Schmidt. Published by Future Horizons. Used with permission.

Other Ideas and Activities for Unit 5

- **Experts for a Day:** This chapter lends itself to Expert for a Day (Unit 3, Lesson 1) because there is a lot of valuable information to share. Encourage each group to concentrate on the big picture and not the details.

- **Debates:** Debates can be used at various times throughout the year, connected to the content of the course or other topics. Non-related topics that the students have enjoyed include presidential candidates, ice cream vs. milkshake, sports team rivalries, summers off vs. year-round school, school uniforms in public schools, etc. Let the students have some input into which side they would like to defend, but it is also good to assign the topic – defending a side you don't actually agree with is a great lesson in TOM (Baron-Cohen et. al., 2013).

- **Role-Play:** After debating whether conflict is good or bad, present a lesson on the different types of fighting styles discussed in Chapter 7, "Resolving Interpersonal Conflict," of *Becoming Aware* (Walker, 2013). Then break students into small groups to create and act out a scenario depicting each type.

Communication Skills

"Thinking alike ...now that's social thinking!" – Mallory

This unit usually falls during the end of third quarter. This is when the progress they are making starts to spill into the students' other classes. Generalization is, of course, the goal of teaching these social communication skills. When Mallory blurted out that thinking alike was "social thinking," I realized she was starting to understand one of the most fundamental and important parts of successful communication. I was so excited about her discovery that I didn't even remind her not to blurt out her comments in class.

In his book *How to Win Friends and Influence People*, Dale Carnegie (1981) quotes Henry Ford as saying that "If there is any one secret of success, it lies in the ability to get the other person's point of view and see things from that person's angle as well as from your own" (p. 35). This skill is also called social thinking (Winner, 2000, 2007) or theory of mind (Baron-Cohen et al., 2013).

Communication skills encompass so much more than what you say and how you say it. Communication has been described as the process of "conveying feelings, attitudes, facts, beliefs and ideas between individuals, either verbally or nonverbally in such a way that the message intended is received" (Walker, 2013, p. 310). People on the autism spectrum struggle to communicate because conveying feelings, reading nonverbals, understanding sarcasm, and perspective taking – major components of communication – are often not innate for them (Hobson, 2012).

This unit allows for intentional teaching of the various skills that make up the whole of communication. It aligns with Chapter 5, "Interpersonal Conflict," of *Becoming Aware* (Walker, 2013); for example, the "Active Listener Checklist" at the end of the chapter is helpful for introducing the importance of active listening. Along with communication and active listening, this unit also stresses the importance of conveying empathy and first impressions. Due to their inherent traits, students on the spectrum need to be taught directly to show their feelings and intentionally show empathy in order to strengthen their interpersonal relationships (Blume & Zembar, 2007).

Finally, in the 21st century, we cannot discuss communication without diving into social media. Many students with ASD are more comfortable connecting with others online than in person, "Because of their social skill deficits, the Internet provides a more fluid means of interacting with peers and opens up the potential pool of social contacts for children with particular disabilities" (Didden et al., 2009, p. 1202).

However, despite their popularity and widespread use, social media pose a number of threats and dangers. For example, according to a poll conducted by *USA Today*, a majority of adults think that online communication is more likely to be misunderstood than a face-to-face conversation (Fare, 2012). While this comes as no surprise to most of us, it does warrant a discussion of when and how to use social media to communicate, especially for students with ASD, who are generally very trusting and can so easily be taken advantage of online. Indeed, this population is a likely target for cyberbullying (Didden et al., 2009). For example, many of my students would never consider that persons they are talking to online may not be who they say they are.

Josh and Lexie working together to complete their Expert's for a Day *project.*

The peer coaches are great resources for this type of discussion because they use social media for a variety of reasons and can help facilitate a discussion about socializing via social media in an age-appropriate way. After all, one of my students recently shared with me that Facebook is Instagram for "old people." Who knew?!

Lessons in Unit 6 include:

- Spaghetti war
- Nonverbal communication
- Take a guess
- Pivot step
- Social media

Survival Skills for the 21st Century Used in This Unit

Critical thinking and problem solving, collaboration across networks and leading by influence, agility and adaptability, accessing and analyzing information, and curiosity and imagination.

(Opening art) The student artist for this chapter was diagnosed with selective mutism, but is now sitting and eating with friends only a year later. Peer involvement is key, and this aspect of PEERspective has made a difference in his life.

Unit 6: Communication Skills
Lesson 1: Spaghetti War

Materials

- Unit 6, Handout 1
- Paper/pens/pencils
- Student journals
- Board
- Tape, 5 straws, 1 box of spaghetti for each group

Duration

One 50-minute class period

Lesson Overview

In this lesson, the teacher basically does not speak for the entire class period but relies on body language. Therefore, the students have to interpret the day's lesson based only nonverbal gestures and facial expressions. Students are divided into small groups and given a box of spaghetti, five straws, and tape. The goal is for the students to use these materials to build the highest structure within the allotted time limit (I usually allow 15 minutes). At the end of the lesson, students complete Unit 6, Handout 1. The next day, the winning structure, is announced and the criteria are shared with the groups.

Student Objectives

1. The students will work in groups to create a structure using spaghetti.
2. The students will work together to decipher the criteria.
3. The students will complete a journal entry.
4. The students will respectfully discuss their thoughts about the journal entry.
5. The students will rely on their group members for guidance and will remain calm even though the teacher will not answer questions or speak at all during the class period.

Rationale

A major trait of ASD is a desire and need for routine and consistency (APA, 2013), and most students on the spectrum, therefore, prefer things to stay the same and become frustrated when things change. In this lesson, the fact that the teacher is giving directions using only nonverbal communication, including and facial expressions, is difficult for the entire class. That is, the students have to rely on the nonverbal communication, reflect on what they decoded, and then wait until the next day for validation – a true test of patience, group dynamics, and perseverance. Students earn points for simply participating in this activity as opposed to a grade for accuracy, and so on.

NPDC Evidence-Based Practices Used in This Lesson

- Cognitive behavioral intervention
- Peer-mediated instruction and intervention
- Self-management
- Modeling

Unit 6, Handout 1

Spaghetti War

Name_____ Date_____

Directions: Work together with your group to determine what the teacher would like you to do. Then, complete the project based on the criteria you think the teacher has communicated to you nonverbally and/or with facial expressions. When you are finished or time is up, please complete the following journal prompt individually. You and the other students will discuss this at the end of class, and the winner of the activity will be announced tomorrow.

Journaling: What are the criteria for this project? How do you know? Did you meet the criteria? How did your group come to this conclusion?

Unit 6: Communication Skills
Lesson 2: Nonverbal Communication

Materials

None

Duration

One 50-minute period

Lesson Overview

Ask the students to sit in a circle. Then pick one student to be the detective. This person goes somewhere where she cannot hear her classmates talking, typically in the hallway outside of the classroom. Ask the remaining students in the room to close their eyes and explain the activity as follows: "I will tap one student on the shoulder, picking him or her to be the 'frog.'" The detective returns to the room and stands in the middle of the circle. The frog tries to stick out its tongue at the students in the circle. If a student makes eye contact with the frog while it is sticking out its tongue, the student must fall to the ground. The detective's job is to determine who the frog is, so the frog needs to be careful not to stick out its tongue when the detective is looking. The detective is allowed three guesses. At the end of the lesson, the students identify takeaways about nonverbal communication.

Student Objectives

1. Students will read nonverbal communication in order to successfully participate in the activity.

2. Students will work together to brainstorm takeaways or the "big picture" ideas/themes about nonverbal communication.

Rationale

Reading nonverbal communication and being aware of your surroundings is an important part of becoming more self-aware. Often people on the spectrum are not aware of those around them, let alone the nonverbal messages they are sending. Most of our communication is nonverbal, so individuals on the autism spectrum are at an obvious disadvantage in this major area of life. We communicate nonverbally much more than verbally in our society, and missing these subtle cues can have a greater impact on communication than many realize. This activity helps students start to recognize and decode nonverbal communication.

NPDC Evidence-Based Practices Used in This Lesson

- Developmental relationship-based treatment
- Peer-mediated instruction and intervention
- Imitation-based interaction
- Self-management

Lesson contributed by Jackie Angioletti, University of Dayton student teacher, 2016.

Unit 6: Communication Skills
Lesson 3: Take a Guess

Materials

- Computer
- Projector
- Paper or student's journal
- Pens/pencil for each student

Duration

One 50-minute class period

Lesson Overview

The students watch a video clip of a Chef Boyardee Whole Grain commercial (https://www. youtube.com/watch?v=16yARJeag4Y) as an example of nonverbal communication that happens in everyday conversations. Afterwards they watch a TV show, typically a soap opera or drama, without sound. The teacher pauses the video clip at regular intervals and the students write down the emotions of different characters, the relationships they have observed through nonverbal communication, and the plot. At the completion of the video clip, the students discuss their observations with a group of 3-4 peers. After the groups have discussed their hypothetical scenarios, students participate in a whole-class discussion and, finally, watch the same clip with sound to see if their predictions were correct.

Student Objectives

1. The students will make educated guesses about what is happening in the video clip and explain why they came to their conclusions.

2. The students will understand and correctly interpret nonverbal communication.

3. The students will discuss their opinions in a respectful way.

Rationale

In the Chef Boyardee Whole Grain commercial, two parents are communicating using only gestures and facial expressions. However, their nonverbal interaction is supplemented with subtitle interpretations of what they are saying to each other, which gives the students a chance to understand what they should be looking for to interpret nonverbal communication. Video modeling is a form of observational learning, in which desired behaviors are demonstrated (NPDC, 2011).

After viewing the commercial, the students identify nonverbal cues in a video, leading to increased awareness of nonverbal communication in daily life. By watching the video clip without sound first, the students are able to focus only on nonverbal communication as the distractions from sound are eliminated. The concluding discussion centers on why they came to certain conclusions and what different nonverbal cues can mean.

NPDC Evidence-Based Practices Used in This Lesson

- Cognitive behavioral intervention
- Computer-aided instruction
- Imitation-based interaction
- Peer-mediated instruction and intervention
- Self-management
- Video modeling

Lesson contributed by Jackie Angioletti, University of Dayton student teacher, 2016.

Unit 6: Communication Skills
Lesson 4: The Pivot Step

Materials
- Board/smartboard
- Internet with video clip
- Recording device

Duration

Two 50-minute class periods (the students start recording their skits toward the end of the first day into the second day. (The second day they present their videos to their peers.)

Lesson Overview

In this lesson, students watch a clip from *Seinfeld* (https://www.youtube.com/watch?v=NGVSIkEi3mM) about the "close talker" and discuss how the characters in the clip must have felt. This leads to a discussion of the fact that different cultures have different expectations regarding proximity between people when having a conversation. In the United States, the preferred distance is about an arm's length. Be sure to explain that this is an estimate, and that you shouldn't reach out your arm to measure this distance each time you talk to someone. Then, demonstrate that if someone is too close to you, you can shift your upper body back and take one step backwards (*pivot step*) so you create more distance without seeming rude. Finish the lesson by having the students get into pairs and practice using Body Basics (Sheridan, 2010) (see Other Ideas and Activities for Unit 6), starting a conversation, and the pivot step. Each pair can demonstrate to the class, or you could have them film what not to do followed by what to do. If you have the students film themselves be sure to allow class time to view the videos. This is a fun way to create social awareness, a shared experience, and integrate video modeling.

Student Objectives

1. The students will watch a *Seinfeld* video clip.
2. The students will discuss how they would feel or have felt in a situation similar to the one in the video clip.
3. The students will learn how to do a "pivot step."
4. The students will work in pairs to practice Body Basics, starting a conversation, and the pivot step.
5. The students will create short videos of what not to do followed by what to do (in that order).
6. The students will view their peers' videos.

Rationale

Nonverbal communication is very important when interacting with others. Sometimes students with ASD do not realize that some of their nonverbal communication can be off-putting to others. For example, proximity when holding a conversation is very important. If a person is closer than expected, it is uncomfortable, and if he is farther away than expected, it can be awkward. Social awareness is a skill that can be taught, and this lesson helps students create parameters to consider when having a conversation with others.

NPDC Evidence-Based Practices Used in This Lesson

- Cognitive behavioral intervention
- Computer-aided instruction
- Imitation-based interaction
- Peer-mediated instruction and intervention

- Scripting
- Social narratives
- Video modeling
- Modeling

Unit 6: Communication Skills
Lesson 5: Social Media

Materials

- Computer access/smartboard
- Student journals
- Pens/pencil for each student

Duration

One 50-minute class period

Lesson Overview

Students will journal on one of the following prompts: "Agree or disagree: Our friends on social media are our friends in real life. Why?" Or, "List five examples of things that are appropriate to post on social media and five that would not be appropriate." After the students have had time to think and respond to the journal prompt, the teacher leads a discussion. Then, the students watch a clip about Internet safety, such as *The Internet Ruined My Life* (syfy.com), described as follows: "… exposes the unexpected perils of living in a social media obsessed world. Each half-hour episode explores what happens to a person when a single tweet, post, or status update backfires and spirals out of control. Told through first person accounts, this series takes stories ripped-from-the-headlines and reveals how people just like you and me inadvertently ruin their lives in one keystroke" (syfy.com). After watching the episode, the students work as a group to compile takeaways and finish the lesson with a discussion.

Student Objectives

1. The students will complete a journal prompt and share their thoughts by contributing to a class discussion.

2. The students will attentively watch an episode of *The Internet Ruined My Life* and take notes.

3. The students will work in small groups to compile 3-5 takeaways.

4. The students will contribute to a whole-class discussion about "takeaways" from the video.

Rationale

A big part of social communication today takes place digitally. While this is a convenient way to communicate in many ways, it has some obvious pitfalls and dangers, especially for students with ASD. This lesson can be delivered several times throughout the year based on students' needs. Each episode deals with a different topic related to digital communication, and the journal prompt can be adjusted to connect to the topic of a given episode. Students on the autism spectrum are easily taken advantage of online, to a great extent due to their literal thinking, which can make them too trusting (Didden et al., 2009). This lesson enables students to see in a black-and-white way the importance of Internet safety.

NPDC Evidence-Based Practices Used in This Lesson	
• Cognitive behavioral intervention	• Self-management
• Computer-aided instruction	• Video modeling
• Peer-mediated instruction and intervention	

Other Ideas and Activities for Unit 6

- **Body Basics:** I have had a lot of success using *The Tough Kid Social Skill Book* (Sheridan, 2010). Although the book is intended for younger students (grades 3-7), there is one idea that I have found to be especially helpful: Body Basics. This is a set formula designed to help students go through a checklist in their heads to ensure that they are following the correct steps in having a conversation. The acronym used to help remember the steps is FEVER:
    Face the other person
    Eye contact
    Voice should be appropriate
    Expression should match what you are saying
    Relax

- **Conversation Skills:** I also use "Starting a Conversation" as well as "Joining In" from *The Tough Kid Social Skills Book* (Sheridan, 2010) throughout the year, but I modify them to make them more appropriate for older students. It is important not to use "juvenile" materials, as these can be off-putting to older students. For example, in "Joining In," the final step is to "ask to join," which I change to "ask a question or make a comment" because that is more age-appropriate for high school students.

- **Role-Play:** When using the Body Basics from *The Tough Kid Social Skills Book* (Sheridan, 2010), I often act out both the correct and the incorrect way of doing the steps or use video clips and allow the students to pick out what was done well and what felt awkward. Video modeling is an effective practice to help students with HFA (Charlop & Milstein, 1989; Charlop, Dennis, Carpenter, & Greenberg, 2010; Marzullo-Kerth, Reeve, Reeve, & Townsend, 2011). If a student continues to struggle with certain skills, you can show them the video of them doing it correctly so they can have the picture in their mind and see themselves doing it the "right" way. Students on the spectrum are often visual learners and thinkers (Dettmer, Simpson, Myles, & Ganz, 2000; Grandin, 1995; Mesibov, 1998; Quill, 1997; Wheeler & Carter, 1998), and I have found video modeling to be one of the most easily implemented and efficient ways to help replace behaviors (Charlop-Christy, Le, & Freeman, 2000).

- **Guest Speakers:** Invite a business professional to speak to the students about the importance of collaboration.

- **Internet Safety:** Invite a police officer to the class to talk about Internet safety and the potential dangers of social media. People with HFA are easy targets for online predators (Kowalski & Fedina, 2011; Sofronoff, Dark, & Stone, 2011) as they tend to be naive and very trusting.

- **Relationship Advice:** Ask a counselor or therapist to speak to the class about how miscommunication and/or lack of communication can create problems in relationships.

- **Self-Assessments:** Chapter 5, "Interpersonal Communication," of *Becoming Aware* (Walker, 2013) includes an assessment to be completed with someone you speak to on a regular basis entitled "Are You an Active Listener?" I use this either at the beginning of this unit or as a wrapup to the unit. It serves as a springboard for a discussion about the importance of active listening.

- **Partner Drawings:** Another fun way to have the students work on their communication skills is to hand them a picture, or several pictures, and ask them to describe it to a partner. The partner is to attempt to draw what is being described without seeing the original picture. This activity is a good lesson not only for teaching communication and listening skills, but also patience – an important lesson in itself. For example, some students get frustrated with how their partner explains how to draw the picture because it is not how they would have said it.

UNIT 7:
Social Etiquette and School Dances

"I'm going to prom, with a date!" – Mal

Each fall I share with the students and their parents that our fourth quarter outing is the school prom. I'm not sure whether the parents or the students are more skeptical about this idea, as attending a dance can be challenging for students on the spectrum with loud music, new atmospheres, and social navigation – not to mention the unfamiliar, itchy clothes and uncomfortable shoes. Thankfully, I've never had a student regret attending.

With each field trip and outing, students build social confidence, which is necessary to be successful participants in the bigger world. Using prom, or any school dance, as a social outing is a key component of our class. Beyond the opportunity for students to have a shared experience that helps them to feel more a part of the school community, such outings allow them to continue to develop social confidence.

While prom is the highlight of fourth quarter (see Appendix 13 for a sample curriculum map for PEERspective), our focus in this unit is not just on the dance, it also enables us to intentionally talk about basic manners and social etiquette. Lack of social awareness (Constantino, Przybeck, Friesen, & Todd, 2000) can impact what students on the spectrum say and how they say it. This, in turn, can result in behavior that is considered rude. It does not matter if a person "means" to be rude or not; once something is said or done, a lasting impact is made. While many students pick up on etiquette and other so-called "hidden curriculum" ideas on their own (Myles, Trautman, & Schelvan, 2013), students with HFA need to be taught explicitly and directly.

Current and past students meeting up at prom.

Temple Grandin, a world-renowned person with autism, attributes a lot of her success to what she calls a "50s upbringing" from her mother – a parenting style invoking teaching moments and inculcating manners, basic social skills, and independence early (MyAutismTeam, 2012). Amid the myriad other things they have to tend to, often, teachers and parents ignore inappropriate behavior, thereby sending the wrong signal to students. That is, by saying nothing, we are giving students the impression that what they are doing or saying is okay. Spending time deliberately discussing appropriate manners and etiquette is necessary to help our students succeed.

Recognizing the importance of abiding by social expectations for polite behavior, many of my students have thanked me for pointing out when their behavior would be considered rude and explaining why.

Joe wrote the following in an essay he submitted to his English teacher at the end of his junior year; the message is clear: As educators and as parents, we cannot assume that students understand the social world around them: "Mrs. Schmidt explained to me that if I didn't take care of my hygiene, it would be a natural barrier to making friends. Why did it take until my junior year for someone to tell me that? I didn't know that it made a difference."

Lessons in Unit 7 include:

- Dance checklist
- Dating dos and don'ts
- Let's dance
- Etiquette lesson/formal dining field trip

Survival Skills for the 21st Century Used in This Unit

Agility and adaptability, initiative and entrepreneurialism, effective oral and written communication, and curiosity and imagination.

(Opening art) Artwork for this chapter was created by Peyton. When I told Peyton she couldn't draw her date as a dog, she creatively found a way around it. Can you tell what her special interest is?

Unit 7: Social Etiquette and School Dances
Lesson 1: Dance Checklist

Materials
- Unit 7, Handout 1
- Pens/pencil for each student
- Paper
- Computer
- Board/smartboard

Duration
Two 50-minute class periods

Lesson Overview
The students work in small groups to create a portion of the dance checklist (i.e., thinking about prom, before prom, during prom, and after prom). Together, the students brainstorm what steps need to be completed or considered during the various phases. After working in their small groups for a day and typing up their checklist, groups take turns presenting their list and getting feedback from their peers. The groups edit their checklist to reflect any of the suggestions made in class. At the end of the second day, the checklists are compiled to create one final document. Finally, each student gets a copy of the final checklist and continues to refer to it throughout the process of preparing for prom.

Student Objectives
1. The students will work together in small groups.
2. The students will contribute what they know about prom and respectfully listen to other group members' opinions.
3. The students will come to a consensus regarding the various steps in the prom checklist.
4. The students will type up the steps.
5. The students will present the steps and revise them as needed.
6. The students will continue to refer to and follow the steps until the dance is over.

Rationale
Each high school has its own traditions with regard to the annual dances. By brainstorming in small groups, students start to think socially about the steps or rules in their school. The final product is a concise list of steps compiled by students who are involved in the school community. This list will serve as a black-and-white structure to this social event, which alleviates some stress and prepares the students for the event.

NPDC Evidence-Based Practices Used in This Lesson
- Cognitive behavioral intervention
- Computer-aided instruction
- Peer-mediated instruction and intervention
- Self-management
- Task analysis

Dance Checklist

Thinking About the Dance

1. Set a budget (3+ weeks ahead)

2. Know the date, time, and place of the event (3+ weeks)

3. Decide if you want to go with a date and/or with a group (3+ weeks)

Before the Dance

☐ Ask a date and/or find a group of friends to go with (PEERspective students have the option of going as a group) (3+ weeks)

☐ Buy your ticket(s) (If bringing a date, talk about paying for the tickets) (2+ weeks)

☐ Find your dress or tux/suit (Coordinate colors with date) (2-3+ weeks)

☐ Arrange for transportation and get directions to events (To date's house, to dinner, to prom, to a location to change clothes, to the after-prom, home) (2-3+ weeks)

☐ Plan for pictures (With date/group? Before or during? Or both?)

☐ Decide on where you will go for dinner (Where? With whom? Who's paying? Do you need reservations?)

☐ Buy flowers; boutonniere (for boys)/corsage (For girl, usually a wrist corsage) (1 week)

☐ Look up the weather forecast and be prepared (Umbrella, jacket, etc.) (1 week, 1 day ahead, etc.)

Day of the Dance

☐ Girls: Hair, makeup, nails (This is optional and you don't have to have all three done) *appointments needed

☐ Guys: Haircut, shave, shower

☐ Pick up flowers (Store in refrigerator!)

☐ Pack a change of comfortable clothes, extra toiletries (Deodorant/perfume, toothbrush/paste, etc.) for after-prom, unless you are going home after the dance

☐ Contact date with any final questions/concerns

During the Dance

- ☐ Hours: 8-11 (most people show up by 9)

- ☐ We will be getting our group picture taken at 9:00, an announcement will be made and we will dance together for a couple songs after our picture.

- ☐ When dancing, have fun, but "keep it at home."

- ☐ Even if you are nervous, no one else has to know. Just smile and relax.

- ☐ If you need a break from the noise, go to the restroom, get a drink of water, or ask Mrs. Schmidt to allow you to step outside for some fresh air. You may only do this with her. Generally, if students leave without permission and try to come back, they are not allowed. But if you are with Mrs. Schmidt, there is an exception to the rule.

After the Dance

- ☐ Post some fun pictures of your experience on social media if you want to.

- ☐ Be proud of yourself; by attending you tried something new and now you have a shared experience with your peers.

- ☐ If you have professional pictures taken, they will make an announcement when they are in and you can pick them up in the main office.

- ☐ If you have any questions while we prepare, either ask in class or put your question in the question box. You will feel much more comfortable if you know what to expect, so please ask!

Unit 7: Social Etiquette and School Dances
Lesson 2: Dating Dos and Don'ts

Materials

- Pens/pencil for each student
- Paper for each student
- Unit 7, Handout 2
- Board/smartboard

Duration

One 50-minute class period

Lesson Overview

Students cut a sheet of paper in half. On one sheet, they write down a dating "do" and on the other, a dating "don't." They lightly crumble each piece into a ball and throw it toward the middle of the room. Then, the papers are read aloud by the teacher, and the students record them on Handout 2. Next, the students view a clip or clips of *How to Lose a Guy in 10 Days* (Petrie, 2003) and add more ideas to Handout 2 based on the movie. The teacher may want to share an explanation of the movie, which is that the male character (Mathew McConaughey) is trying to make the female character (Kate Hudson) fall in love with him, while the female character is trying to cause him to break up with her. After Unit 7, Handout 2, is completed, students discuss it in a small group.

Student Objectives

1. The students will take part in a whole-class discussion about dating.

2. The students will watch a video clip and write down "dos" and "don'ts."

3. The students will share their final lists with a small group.

Rationale

Discussing appropriate dating behavior before a dance can be very helpful. It is usually much easier to pick out social mistakes in someone else's behavior than recognizing it in our own. Due to lack of social awareness, many students on the spectrum have difficulty knowing if their behavior is inappropriate (Iovannone, Dunlap, Huber, & Kincaid, 2003). By using a video clip, especially one that shows exaggerated behaviors, students can learn to pick out "dos" and don'ts." This lesson is a good way to create parameters for expected dating behavior. In addition, opening the lesson with an anonymous brainstorm of "dos" and "don'ts" allows the teacher to see where the baseline knowledge is. This can then help to guide the concluding discussion of the lesson.

NPDC Evidence-Based Practices Used in This Lesson
- Cognitive behavioral intervention
- Imitation-based interaction
- Peer-mediated instruction and intervention
- Self-management
- Social narratives
- Video modeling

Dating: Dos and Don'ts

Name_____ Date_____

Based on the class discussion and the video clip(s) from the movie *How to Lose a Guy in 10 Days* (Petrie, 2003), please record your dating "dos" and "don'ts" (as many as you can list) in the space provided.

Dating "Dos"

Dating "Don'ts"

Unit 7: Social Etiquette and School Dances
Lesson 3: Let's Dance!

Materials

- Computer – YouTube
- Smartboard/TV
- Music

Duration

One 50-minute period (more time the next day may be needed)

Lesson Overview

Start this lesson with a discussion about dancing. Be sure to mention that (a) it is optional, (b) students can dance with their date and/or a group of friends, (c) students don't have to be great dancers to try it, and (d) it is best to keep the movements small and basic, especially if they have never danced before. Remind the students that, in any given social situation, if they are unsure of what to do, they should look around and see what the majority of those around them are doing and try to imitate that.

Then show a clip from the movie *Hitch* (Lassiter et. al., 2005; https://www.youtube.com/watch?v=2bH0OXsmsbQ). Stop the clip at 1:21 to discuss the concept of keeping it at "home," which means keeping one's dance movements small. Then, have a pre-chosen peer coach play a fast-paced, school-appropriate song and ask the other students to dance and help each other minimize any movements that would look out of place. Remind the coaches to be honest but kind and to offer specific suggestions. Repeat with a popular slow song – having two peer coaches demonstrate the appropriate way to participate in a basic slow dance. End with a discussion of takeaways.

Student Objectives

1. The students will become familiar with expectations regarding dancing at prom.
2. The students will review social thinking (Winner, 2000, 2007) and discuss expected/unexpected behavior (Winner, 2000, 2007).
3. The students will practice dancing to both fast and slow music with peer coaches.
4. The students will brainstorm takeaways and share them in a whole-class discussion.

Rationale

In order to help students to feel comfortable at prom, all aspects of the evening should be addressed, including dancing. The students will be more likely to have a positive memory of dancing if they are taught age-appropriate dance moves by their peers than by the teacher. By playing current music, the students will practice dancing to songs that may be played at the prom. Social awareness is reinforced by discussing small dance movements and reminding students to look at those around them for social cues.

NPDC Evidence-Based Practices Used in This Lesson
- Computer-aided instruction
- Developmental relationship-based treatment
- Imitation-based interaction
- Peer-mediated instruction and intervention
- Social narratives
- Modeling

Unit 7: Social Etiquette and School Dances
Lesson 4: Etiquette Lesson/Formal Dining Field Trip

Materials

None

Duration

Length of the field trip with 30-minute follow-up the next school day

Lesson Overview

This lesson is our fourth-quarter (see Appendix 13) field trip. The students are required to dress up, and are paired for a "mock date." Contact a formal dining establishment to set up a dining etiquette lesson. The local restaurant that does our lesson is family-owned. The owner designs a menu that includes a four-course meal with different options for beverage, appetizer, main course, and dessert. She then teaches an etiquette lesson in between the courses, showing how to pull out the date's chair (if the guy), where to place the napkin, utensil use, proper ordering, basic table manners, and much more. If you cannot find a restaurant owner who is willing to accommodate, you can do this in your classroom with the help of parent volunteers.

Student Objectives

1. The students will dress up.

2. The students will interact with their "date."

3. The students will order and pay for themselves.

4. The students will listen to the etiquette lesson.

5. The students will ask and answer questions.

6. The students will practice appropriate table manners.

Rationale

Again, this unit is all about helping the students to become more socially aware and preparing them for the shared experience of the school dance. By practicing in an authentic setting, the students become more comfortable and socially aware in preparation for the night of the dance and future outings of their own. Having someone who is in the restaurant business share this information creates buy-in. Pairing the students up for "mock dates" allows them to experience being on a date. This field trip focuses on trying something new in a safe environment. Many students have reported that this unit, in particular this field trip, enabled them to be more confident on the big night and also on any dates or other formal social occasions in the future.

NPDC Evidence-Based Practices Used in This Lesson

- Developmental relationship-based treatment
- Imitation-based interaction
- Peer-mediated instruction and intervention
- Self-management
- Modeling

Other Ideas and Activities for Unit 7

- **Authentic Practice:** On the dance night, I take the PEERspective prom group back to the same restaurant where we had our etiquette lesson.

- **Role-Play:** Role-play/drama can be helpful when prepping for field trips and outings. Things like asking someone to the dance, small talk, and meeting your date's parents are just a few of the possibilities.

- **Hidden Curriculum:** Don't assume that the students know the unwritten social rules of your school environment. Be sure to explain proper attire for the dance, that students can go with or without a date, how to buy tickets, etc.

- **Group Memories:** Take a group photo at the dance so that the students can remember the night.

- **Shared Experiences:** We make a special request for a PEERspective song for the class to dance together. This ensures that the students dance at least once!

- **Question Box:** Have a question box in the classroom so that students can ask questions anonymously. This can be used all year, but is especially helpful before big events. As the students become more socially aware, they may shy away from asking questions about things they think everyone else knows, so they can use the question box without anybody knowing.

UNIT 8:
Life Transitions

"I've been growing up my whole life." – Jesse

It made me laugh out loud when Jesse proclaimed that he'd been growing up his whole life. There is something interesting about an 18-year-old discussing his "whole life," but he's right. The 18 years leading up to his senior year have prepared him for his future. I sincerely hope that the intentional social skills training, including this culminating unit on life transitions, has equipped Jesse and other students to find the success and fulfillment they deserve.

This final unit focuses on helping students manage life transitions. Occurring at the end of the school year, the unit ends with a mock job interview as a final exam – what better way to assess growth than to see if the students are able to take the past nine months of social intervention and put it to use?

Transitions are difficult for many students on the autism spectrum (Smith, Barker, Seltzer, Abbeduto, & Greenberg, 2012). If anxiety, to a large extent, is fear of the unknown, it is no wonder transitions are difficult and intimidating. By teaching students that their internal dialogue has a lot to do with future success and helping them gain social confidence through content mastery, we can rest assured that they will be less anxious when they are faced with a new adventure. The future should be exciting, not intimidating.

Generally, PEERspective is offered to students in their junior and senior years. But one year, I made an exception for a sophomore, Alyssa. Her mom insisted that Alyssa could not handle another year of misinterpreted social interactions and having few, if any, friends, so I agreed to let Alyssa join the class. Throughout the year I had mixed feelings about this decision and often wondered if I had made the right choice, but my fears were allayed one day when Alyssa handed me an essay she had written about why it was important that all schools offer PEERspective:

"My social skills improved after participating in PEERspective at the high school. We were taught to be socially competent in group projects, and eventually job interviews. Both group projects and job interviews required people to be polite and show propriety, because they wanted people to be respectful of others. PEERspective allowed me to feel part of the community, because it gave me an opportunity to speak up in conversations, especially during tough situations. When I decided to talk in a conversation, I was understood and listened to. Overall, my transition from childhood to adulthood was marked by my participation in PEERspective".

While it is always good to hear from your students that what you are teaching is making a difference, this particular interaction meant even more to me. Sometimes it's hard to tell exactly what impact the class has made, but know that your work will make a difference.

Lessons in Unit 8 include:

- The dash

- Interest survey

- Mock interview/final exam

Survival Skills for the 21st Century Used in this Unit

Critical thinking and problem solving, effective oral and written communication, accessing and analyzing information, and curiosity and imagination.

(Opening art) The student artist for this chapter chose to stay anonymous. Many of my students are very talented artists, but they do not like to share their artwork or take credit for it. This student made me this picture of a sunflower, which is my favorite flower, as a gift. I'm thankful for these thoughtful and kind individuals I get to work with every day.

Unit 8: Life Transitions
Lesson 1: The Dash

Materials

- Unit 8, Handout 1
- Computer – YouTube/music
- Student journals
- Pens/pencil for each student
- Smartboard/TV

Duration

Two 50-minute class periods, one to complete the lesson and the next day to share and discuss

Lesson Overview

Play *The Dash* (McCreery, 2013; https://www.youtube.com/watch?v=JYlLtTMcnoM) and ask the students to get out their journals and write down their thoughts about it. After the students listen to the song and record their thoughts, have a group discussion about what they wrote in their journals.

Then, ask the students to complete Unit 8, Handout 1, individually. This lesson is very abstract and can be challenging for students with ASD. If students are struggling, consider allowing them to work in small groups or give an example of what your own dash would look like. The next day, allow the students to work with a partner and present a selection of the events they listed on their dash. As a follow-up, encourage students to share their dash with their parents.

Student Objectives

1. The students will listen to the song *The Dash* and write down their thoughts and feelings.
2. The students will contribute to a discussion.
3. The students will complete Unit 8, Handout 1.
4. The students will practice presenting their dash with a partner.
5. The students will present their dash to the class.

Rationale

In order to know what your life's plan is, it is necessary to take time to reflect on what you hope to accomplish. This lesson encourages the students to do that while navigating the abstract nature of their future. Sharing their goals with others gives them validity and allows them to start thinking about the future and why upcoming transitions, such as graduation and future schooling and/or work, are important. Trying to imagine the end result can help students understand why they need to push themselves to do things that they find difficult. Having the students share their dash with their parents can open up a dialogue on what the future brings and what support the students will need to meet their goals.

NPDC Evidence-Based Practices Used in This Lesson
• Computer-aided instruction
• Developmental relationship-based treatment
• Peer-mediated instruction and intervention
• Self-management

The Dash

After listening to *The Dash* (McCreery, 2013) and recording your thoughts in your journal, please develop your own dash and write it below. The dash is a symbol of what you hope to accomplish in your life. This is not meant to be morbid, but to help you find direction and clarity as we discuss life transitions. Please include no less than eight events on your dash and use the space below the dash to explain each event. You will choose 3-5 events to share with your classmates on presentation day.

My Dash: _____

1)

2)

3)

4)

5)

6)

7)

8)

9)

Unit 8: Life Transitions
Lesson 2: Interest Survey

Materials

- Unit 8, Handout 2
- Pens/pencil for each student

Duration

One 50-minute class period, with time at home to conduct the interview and follow-up questions

Lesson Overview

Students complete an interest survey (Unit 8, Handout 2) about where they see themselves years from now and how they plan to get there. The lesson begins with a homework assignment requesting the students to ask a parent or other trusted adult if they are where they thought they would be based on their goals and dreams as a high school student (question 1, Unit 8, Handout 1). In class, discuss their findings. Then, have the students answer all the questions on Unit 8, Handout 1, individually. Students on the spectrum may need prompting to not over-think their answers and remember that they are "guessing" based on their current interests and desires. In groups, students discuss what they put down on their paper and give honest feedback. The lesson ends with a whole-class discussion and another brief homework assignment to discuss Unit 8, Handout 2, with parents or the trusted adult the students first interviewed. The completed handout is turned in the next day with an optional follow-up discussion.

Student Objectives

1. The students will ask a parent and/or trusted adult question 1 on Unit 8, Handout 2.
2. The students will participate in a discussion about their findings on question 1.
3. The students will answer all of the questions on the survey form.
4. The students will accept and provide honest feedback to their peers in a small-group discussion.
5. The students will participate in a whole-class discussion about Unit 8, Handout 2.
6. The students will ask a follow-up question to the parent or trusted adult they first spoke to.

Rationale

This unit is designed to help students consider what their goals are and where they "see" themselves years from now. This can be difficult, especially for students on the spectrum, due to its abstract nature. This lesson not only gives the students an opportunity to reflect on their future, it also opens up a dialogue with parents and/or a trusted adult, allowing the adults to learn what the student is thinking and help them support the student. The questions that the students ask adults are designed to help them see that it is rare for someone to be exactly where they thought they would be, and that it's okay. This realization can help alleviate some stress and create an open dialogue with an adult they trust if and when changes occur in the future. This form can also be helpful when writing IEP goals related to transition and future planning.

NPDC Evidence-Based Practices Used in This Lesson	
• Computer-aided instruction	• Peer-mediated instruction and intervention
• Developmental relationship-based treatment	• Self-management

Interest Survey/Future Planning

Name: _____   Date: _____

Ask a trusted adult and/or parent this question and record your answer.

1. When you were my age, where did you think you would be at your current age? Please tell me about where you thought you would be and where you are in your life now.

The following questions will be completed during class time:

1. If I go to college, I plan to study/after high school, I will …

2. In five years I see myself …

3. In 10 years, I will be …

4. In 20 years, I will be (don't say "old") …

5. After you complete the above questions, ask the person whom you asked question 1 to respond to the following:

   Looking at the answers I wrote above, what are your thoughts? What advice do you have for me? Do you think that my plans fit my natural talents?

Unit 8: Life Transitions
Lesson 3: Mock Interviews

Materials

- Volunteer interviewers
- Pens/pencil for each student
- Student journals
- Unit 8, Handouts 3, 4, and 5

Duration

This lesson is designed for a 2½-hour exam period. (It can be adjusted into three class periods if needed.)

Lesson Overview

This lesson can be used as a final exam or as a stand-alone lesson that will take several consecutive days. The first day, start class with a journal prompt that gets the students thinking about what is important when being interviewed. Then, begin a class discussion about interviewing skills. Finally, have the students work in pairs to formulate possible interview questions and take turns role-playing using these questions.

The next day, students take turns completing a mock interview. In order to make it authentic, invite small-business owners, people who work in human relations, and principals and/or administrators to conduct the interviews. Each student interview should last about 15 minutes. Provide each interviewer with a list of the same questions with a rubric for grading. You may want to remind the interviewer that constructive and honest feedback can be very helpful to the students. Finish the class with a panel of all of the interviewers and ask them to discuss things that they thought most of the students did well and areas to improve. The panelists should discuss the students as a whole and not pick out specific students. The class concludes with student questions for the interviewers.

Student Objectives

1. The students will complete a journal entry about interviewing skills.
2. The students will work in pairs to compile a list of possible interview questions.
3. The students will role-play an interview with their partner.
4. The students will participate in a mock interview and follow the guidelines given.
5. The students will listen to and ask questions to the panel of interviewers.

Rationale

This lesson is a culmination of all the work done throughout the year in PEERspective. The students will need to use perspective taking, demonstrate appropriate nonverbal skills, communicate effectively, and leave their interviewer with positive thoughts about them.

NPDC Evidence-Based Practices Used in This Lesson

- Imitation-based interaction
- Naturalistic intervention
- Peer-mediated instruction and intervention
- Scripting
- Self-management

PEERspective: Final Exam

Pre- and Post-Interview Reflections

Please take a few minutes to complete the pre-questions while you are waiting for your turn to be interviewed and then complete the post-questions after you have completed your interview.

Pre-Interview Question

How are you feeling about being interviewed? Are you nervous? What is your "game plan" for this interview and how have you prepared?

Post-Interview Questions

How did you feel the interview went today? What did you do well and what could/should you improve on in the future? Do you think you left the interviewer with a positive or neutral feeling about you? How could you tell and what did you do to ensure that you are "hired"? What are your takeaways from this experience?

Mock Interview Questions

1. What personality traits do you have that would help you in this job?

2. What skills do you currently possess that would make you a good fit for this position?

3. Give an example of a time when you demonstrated one of the skills/traits you have previously mentioned.

4. What area two accomplishments in your life that you are most proud of?

5. What are three important things you want me to know about you?

6. What would be the most difficult thing for you to do in this job? How will you be able to overcome this?

7. Give a specific example of a time when you used good judgment and logic in solving a problem.

8. Give a specific occasion in which you conformed to a policy with which you did not agree.

9. What questions do you have for me at this time?

Mock Interview Rubric

Student's Name: _____ Date Completed: _____

_____/10 points: Appearance: Dress appropriately for the interview.

_____/5 points: Greeting/Introduction: We recommend that you stand to greet your interviewer with a handshake, using his/her name. Also, make good eye contact with the interviewer, smile, and be professional.

_____/5 points: Body Language: During the interview, be aware of your eye contact, subtle use of hands while speaking, good posture, etc.

_____/15 points: Attitude: Your attitude toward work and working with others is crucial in the hiring process. Be sure to convey an attitude that is enthusiastic, sincere, and genuine.

_____/40 points: Responses to the Interview Questions: Do your research and practice, practice, practice! Know your goals and be able to express them to the interviewer.

_____/20 points: Oral Communication: Speak clearly and concisely. Try to think out your response before answering a question.

_____/5 points: Preparation: Prepare questions for your interviewer and research the position and/or company/organization/agency for which you are interviewing. It is important to have knowledge on the particular program and be able to articulate why you want to further your education in that field.

_____/100

Positive Aspects:

Areas of Need/Continued Growth:

Other Comments:

Other Ideas and Activities for Unit 8

- **Guest Speakers:** Invite a human relations professional to be a guest speaker to talk about what companies look for in future job candidates and give advice on writing résumés and communicating effectively in job interviews.

- **Reflect:** Create a lesson or assign a journal prompt dealing with a past experience students have had with a transition and the feelings associated with it. This will allow the students to reflect on the fact that they have gone through these events in the past successfully.

- **Video Modeling:** Utilize video modeling whereby the students act out and record skits dealing with transition and/or change with a positive outcome.

- **Job Shadow:** Have the students job shadow somebody in an area that interests them.

Encore

"Less like a turtle." – Dr. Joe

Joe was placed in my study skills class not because he needed any academic support, but because study hall was his "personal hell." For the first few weeks, I was fairly certain that Joe was plotting my demise because he appeared to be miserable. How wrong I was! I am so thankful that he was willing to help me pilot PEERspective all those years ago. When asked about the impact of the class at the end of the first year, Joe responded, "Well, I definitely feel less like a turtle."

Joe's comment about feeling "less like a turtle" has resonated with me as the perfect analogy for how many students with ASD feel – hidden in a shell, afraid to poke their heads into the social world. But I am happy to report that over the years, I have seen my students, little by little, bravely push themselves outside their comfort zones.

In this chapter you will find additional activities that can be used in conjunction with the foundational eight units to help your students push themselves out of their comfort zones. Some of the activities may seem less than academic, but they encourage the students to work as a group towards a common goal, or to do activities they may not attempt on their own. As educators, it is our job to continue thinking outside the box to create learning opportunities that allow our students to have positive experiences in the social world.

Pop Culture

Most students on the spectrum whom I have worked with have little desire to stay up on pop culture or what's "trending." While I understand their perspective, in terms of the lack of importance and validity of these things in their lives, the students are missing out on an opportunity to connect socially.

Using pop culture or trending topics as journal prompts will help inform your students about popular topics and, in the process, possibly prevent them from saying things like "Beyoncé who?" in response to a peer's question about the popular singer. While we don't need for them to unravel the mystery that a student posed of "What is a Kardashian?," it can help students socialize if they have some clue about things like the upcoming Super Bowl, popular movies, YouTube clips, memes, and yes, even some celebrity news.

Holidays

Fun lessons can be created around holidays and special events at your school emphasizing cooperative learning opportunities. Examples include putting together holiday puzzles, creating ginger bread houses, or carving pumpkins.

To illustrate, when carving pumpkins, I break the students into groups so they work as a team. The groups have one class period to decide on a design and carve their pumpkins, which are then judged, and a winner is crowned. Also around Halloween, I do a mini-lesson on sarcasm using a book written by Jerry Seinfeld entitled *Halloween* (Seinfeld, 2008). Other holiday ideas include a Secret Santa gift exchange (or change the name to fit any season (e.g., Secret Cupid), which allows students to practice perspective taking. Overall, holidays by their very nature offer many opportunities for students to practice social skills.

Talent Show

Our annual school talent show – a highly anticipated and much talked-about event – is another exciting opportunity for the students to become involved in the school community. At our high school there are 2,800 students, so making it into the talent show is quite an accomplishment. With the PEERspective students, we use a popular song and create a "flash mob" style dance that all students participate in. The students dance in the audience so they are not as nervous as they would be on stage, and we usually pass out something to the audience (necklaces, hats, or other props) to get them involved. When the music stops, we sit down and act like nothing happened. Many of our students have not been involved in after-school activities where their parents could come support them, and certainly nothing like this. By dancing in the talent show, even in the audience, not only are they pushing themselves outside their comfort zone, they are now a part of an act that was well received and will be talked about for a while. This helps to bond the students and also builds social confidence.

Social Media

Social media play a large role in teens' social lives these days. Embracing this concept, we use social media in a variety of ways in our class. In a practical manner, we use the app Remind to share information about upcoming events with students and parents. Beyond that, we have found that a student-run Instagram account that students and parents can follow is a great way to cultivate friendships and show the parents how much fun we are having in class. Furthermore, parents can see what skills are being practiced in class, which can cultivate discussions and reinforcement of these things at home.

Movies/TV

Use movies and video clips when possible. It's much easier for students to pick out issues when they see others doing it rather than seeing it in themselves. Also, movies, especially animated ones, are usually filled with overdramatizing.

- *Big Bang Theory* – Many of the characters in this show struggle to relate socially and fail to understand social nuances, figurative language, and sarcasm.

- *Liar, Liar* – In this movie, Jim Carey's character can't lie. This is an interesting way to discuss "white lies" or social fakes. The film also shows the ramifications of not filtering your thoughts. I recommend using clips only due to some of the film's content.

- *Autism in Love* – This film follows several couples with autism who have fallen in love

- Animated films such as *Shrek, Tangled, Inside Out* – These films can be useful to teach emotions, nonverbal communication, and relationships, among other things.

Final Thoughts

A parent of one of my students once told me, "I didn't think my son would ever go to prom, and he did – with a date! These types of exposures wouldn't have happened without the support of PEERspective." Another parent felt similarly, explaining that after our class, her daughter seemed much more aware of other people, their opinions, and what they might be feeling.

Teachers have reported improvements as well, providing evidence that the students are starting to generalize the skills: "I feel that PEERspective has a lot to do with my student's confidence and preparedness, as she has started to approach me with questions and concerns." A special educator stated, "Individuals on my caseload who took the class benefitted significantly in the development of their social and communication skills."

But most important, the students themselves are recognizing the results. "So, I am here to tell you how important this class is. I was a student last year, and the peers really helped me to understand some things I struggled with." Another target student noted that she had never been to the mall without her parents and that going with friends from class made her feel "independent." The lasting impacts are not just on the students with HFA. On average, one third of our peer coaches decide to go into the field of special education. One coach commented, "Seeing their faces when they figure something out can make your whole day." Another commented on how the class helped him personally, saying, "This class has helped me see my weaknesses while being able to truly help other students that need it." Realizing the benefits this class has for all students, it is my hope that through emphasizing pragmatic language skills and working closely with our students, this new approach can help bridge the social gap for some extraordinary individuals.

(Opening artwork) Artwork for this chapter was created by a very special young lady named Corinne Schmidt, who happens to be my youngest daughter. Corinne, her older sister, Elyse, and my husband, Brad, are often involved in PEERspective social outings. Actually, many of my family members have joined us on our outings, and I can't thank them enough for their love and support.

References

Alberto, P. A., Cihak, D. F., & Gama, R. I. (2005). Use of static picture prompts versus video modeling during simulation instruction. *Research in Developmental Disabilities, 26,* 327-339.

Alwell, M., & Cobb, B. (2009). A map of the intervention literature in secondary special education transition. *Career Development for Exceptional Individuals, 29,* 3-27.

American Psychiatric Association. (2013). *Diagnostic and statistical manual of mental disorders* (5th ed.). Washington, DC: Author.

American Psychological Association. (2016). *Exercise fuels the brain's stress buffers.* Retrieved from http://www.apa.org/helpcenter/exercise-stress.aspx

Apple, A. L., Billingsley, F., & Schwartz, I. S. (2005). Effects of video modeling alone and with self-management on compliment-giving behaviors of children with high-functioning ASD. *Journal of Positive Behavior Interventions, 7,* 33-46.

Aspy, R., & Myles, B.S. (2016). *High-functioning autism and difficult moments.* Future Horizons.

Bandura, A. (1977a). Self-efficacy: Toward a unifying theory of behavioral change. *Psychological Review, 84*(2), 191-215.

Bandura, A. (1977b). *Social learning theory.* Upper Saddle River, NJ: Prentice Hall.

Bandura, A. (1993). Perceived self-efficacy in cognitive development and functioning. *Educational Psychologist, 28*(2), 117-148.

Baron-Cohen, S., Tager-Flusberg, H., & Lombardo, M. (Eds.). (2013). *Understanding other minds: Perspectives from developmental social neuroscience.* Oxford University Press.

Bass, J. D., & Mulick, J. A. (2007). Social play skill enhancement of children with autism using peers and siblings as therapists. *Psychology in the School, 44,* 727-734.

Bates, P. E., Cuvo, T., Miner, C. A., & Korabeck, C. A. (2001). Simulated and community-based instruction involving persons with mild and moderate mental retardation. *Research in Developmental Disabilities, 22,* 95-115.

Bellini, S. (2006). *Building social relationships: A systematic approach to teaching social interaction skills to children and adolescents with autism spectrum disorders and other social difficulties.* Shawnee Mission, KS: Autism Asperger Publishing Co.

Bellini, S., & Akullian, J. (2007). A meta-analysis of video modeling and video self-modeling interventions for children and adolescents with autism spectrum disorders. *Exceptional Children, 73,* 264-287.

Bellini, S., Peters, J., Brenner, L., & Hopf, A. (2007). A meta-analysis of school-based social skills interventions for children with autism spectrum disorders. *Remedial and Special Education, 28,* 153-162.

Blume, L. B., & Zembar, M. J. (2007). *Middle childhood to middle adolescence: Development from ages 8 to 18.* Upper Saddle River, NJ: Pearson Education, Inc.

Bright, T., Bittick, K., & Fleeman, B. (1981). Reduction of self-injurious behavior using sensory integrative techniques. *American Journal of Occupational Therapy, 35,* 167-172.

Carnegie, D. (1981). *How to win friends and influence people.* New York, NY: Simon & Schuster.

Charlop, M. H., Dennis, B., Carpenter, M. H., & Greenberg, A. L. (2010). Teaching socially expressive behaviors to children with autism through video modeling. *Education and Treatment of Children, 33,* 371-393.

Charlop, M. H., & Milstein, J. P. (1989). Teaching autistic children conversational speech using video modeling. *Journal of Applied Behavior Analysis, 22,* 275-285. doi:10.1901/jaba.1989.22-275

Charlop-Christy, M. H., Le, L., & Freeman, K. A. (2000). A comparison of video modeling with in vivo modeling for teaching children with autism. *Journal of Autism and Developmental Disorders, 30,* 537-552.

Cihak, D., Alberto, P. A., Taber-Doughty, T., & Gama, R. I. (2006). A comparison of static picture prompting and video prompting simulation strategies using group instructional procedures. *Focus on Autism and Other Developmental Disabilities, 21,* 89-99.

Constantino, J. N., Przybeck, T., Friesen, D., & Todd, R. D. (2000). Reciprocal social behavior in children with and without pervasive developmental disorders. *Journal of Behavioral Pediatrics, 21,* 2-11.

Denham, S., Mason, T., Caverly, S., Schmidt, M., Hackney, R., Caswell, C., & Demulder, E. (2001). Preschoolers at play: Cosocializers of emotional and social competence. *International Journal of Behavioral Development, 25,* 290-301.

Dettmer, S., Simpson, R. L., Myles, B. S., & Ganz, J. B. (2000). The use of visual supports to facilitate transitions of students with autism. *Focus on Autism and Other Developmental Disabilities, 15,* 163-169.

Didden, R., Scholte, R. H., Korzilius, H., DeMoor, J. M., Vermeulen, A., O'Reilly, M., . . . Lancioni, G. E. (2009). Cyberbullying among student with intellectual and developmental disability in special education settings. *Developmental Neurorehabilitation, 12,* 146-151.

Doran, G. T. (1981). There's a S.M.A.R.T. way to write management's goals and objectives. *Management Review, 70*(11), 35-36. Retrieved from https://www.projectsmart.co.uk/brief-history-of-smart-goals.php

Eaves, L. C., & Ho, H. (2008). Young adult outcome of autism spectrum disorders. *Journal of Autism and Developmental Disorders, 38,* 739-747.

Endow, J. (2016, August 2). *Autism, social greetings and rhetorical questions.* Retrieved from http://www.judyendow.com/autistic-behavior/autism-social-greetings-and-rhetorical-questions/

Evans, R., Obst, L., & Peters, C. (Producers), & Petrie, D. (Director). (2003). *How to lose a guy in 10 days* [Motion picture]. Los Angeles, CA: Paramount Pictures.

Fare, E. K. (2012, April 29). *Facebook can't replace face to face conversations.* Retrieved from https://usatoday30.usatoday.com/news/opinion/forum/story/2012-04-29/facebook-face-to-face/54629816/1

Fenaughty, J. (2014). *Game-based strategies implementation during social skills training for non-elementary aged individuals* (Doctoral dissertation, University of Central Florida). Retrieved from http://stars.library.ucf.edu/cgi/viewcontent.cgi?article=5532&context=etd

Ferguson, S. (Producer), & Jackson, M. (Director). (2010). *Temple Grandin* [Motion picture]. Los Angeles, CA: Austin Studios.

Fisher, N., & Happé, F. (2006). A training study of theory of mind and executive functions in children with autism spectrum disorder. *Journal of Autism and Developmental Disorders, 35,* 757-771.

Folkman, Z. (2013). *Zenger Folkman research uncovers how to not get fired* [Press release]. Retrieved from http://www.prnewswire.com/news-releases/zenger-folkman-research-uncovers-how-to-not-get-fired-225040792.html

Ganz, J., Heath, A., Lund, E., Camargo, S., Rispoli, M., Boles, M., & Plaisance, L. (2012). Effects of peer-mediated implementation of visual scripts in middle school. *Behavior Modification, 36,* 378-398.

Geller, L. (2005, Summer). Emotional regulation in autism spectrum disorders. *Autism Spectrum Quarterly,* 14-17.

Gordon, T. (2000). *Parent effectiveness training.* New York, NY: New American Library.

Grandin, T. (1995). How people with autism think. In E. Schopler & G. Mesibov (Eds.), *Learning and cognition in autism: Current issues in autism* (pp. 137-156). New York, NY: Plenum.

Grandin, T (2010, January/February). The need to be perfect. *Autism Asperger's Digest.* Retrieved from http://autismdigest.com/the-need-to-be-perfect/

Gresham, F. M., Sugai, G., & Horner, R. H. (2001). Interpreting outcomes of social skills training for students with high-incidence disabilities. *Teaching Exceptional Children, 67,* 331-344.

Hart, K. J., & Morgan, J. R. (1993). *Cognitive behavior procedures with children and adolescents: A practical guide.* Boston, MA: Allyn Bacon.

Hebron, J., & Humphrey, N. (2014). Exposure to bullying among students with autism spectrum conditions: A multi-informant analysis of risk and protective factors. *Autism, 18*(6), 618-630.

Hobson, R. P. (2012). Autism, literal language and concrete thinking: Some developmental considerations. *Metaphor and Symbol, 27,* 4-21.

Humphrey, N., & Symes, W. (2010). Perceptions of social support and experiences of bullying among pupils with autism spectrum disorders (ASD) in mainstream secondary schools. *European Journal of Special Needs Education, 25,* 77-91.

Iovannone, R., Dunlap, G., Huber, H., & Kincaid, D. (2003). Effective educational practices for students with autism spectrum disorders. *Focus on Autism and Other Developmental Disabilities, 18*(3), 150-165.

Kientz, M. A., & Dunn, W. (1997). A comparison of the performance of children with and without autism on the sensory profile. *The American Journal of Occupational Therapy, 51,* 530-537.

Koul, R. K., Schlosser, R. W., & Sancibrian, S. (2001). Effects of symbol, referent, and instructional variables on the acquisition of aided and unaided symbols by individuals with autism spectrum disorders. *Focus on Autism and Other Developmental Disabilities, 16,* 162-169.

Kowalski, R. M., & Fedina, C. (2011). Cyber bullying in ADHD and Asperger syndrome populations. *Autism Spectrum Disorders, 5,* 1201-1208.

Lassiter, J., Smith, W., & Zee, T. (Producers), & Tennant, A. (Director). (2005). *Hitch* [Motion picture]. Los Angeles, CA: Sony Publishing.

Laushey, K. M., & Heflin, L. J. (2000). Enhancing social skills of kindergarten children with autism through the training of multiple peers as tutors. *Journal of Autism and Developmental Disorders, 30,* 183-193.

Loveland, K. A., & Tunali-Kotoski, B. (2005). The school-age child with an autistic spectrum disorder. In F. R. Volkmar, R. Paul, A. Klin, & D. Cohen (Eds.), *Handbook of autism and pervasive developmental disorders: Diagnosis, development, neurobiology and behavior* (Vol. 1, pp. 247-287). Hoboken, NJ: Wiley.

Luft, J. (1969). *Of human interaction.* Houston, TX: Mayfield Publishing Company.

March, J., & Mulle, K. (1998). *OCD in children and adolescents: A cognitive behavioral treatment manual.* New York, NY: Guilford Press.

Marzano, R. J. (2012). Art and science of teaching/The many uses of exit slips. *Students Who Challenge Us, 70*(2), 80-81. Retrieved from http://www.ascd.org/publications/educational-leadership/oct12/vol70/num02/The-Many-Uses-of-Exit-Slips.aspx

Marzullo-Kerth, D., Reeve, S. A., Reeve, K. F., & Townsend, D. B. (2011). Using multiple-exemplar training to teach a generalized repertoire of sharing to children with autism. *Journal of Applied Behavior Analysis, 44,* 279-294. doi:10.1901/jaba.2011.44-279

McCreery, S. (2013). The dash. On *See You Tonight* [CD]. New York, NY: Sony/ATV Music Publishing LLC.

Merrell, K. W., & Gimpel, G. A. (1998). *Social skills of children and adolescents: Conceptualization, assessment, treatment.* Mahwah, NJ: Lawrence Erlbaum Associates.

Mesibov, G. B. (1998). *Learning styles of students with autism.* Retrieved from http://www.autism-society.org/packages/edkids_learning-styles.html

Mills, N., Pajares, F., & Heron, C. (2007). SES of college intermediate French students: Relation to achievement and motivation. *Language Learning, 57*(3), 417-442.

Morrison, R. S., & Blackburn, A. M. (2008). Take the challenge: Building social competency in adolescents with Asperger's syndrome. *TEACHING Exceptional Children Plus, 5*(2).

MyAutismTeam. (2012, July 11). *Temple Grandin on the importance of giving kids with autism a "50's upbringing"* [Web log post]. Retrieved from https://www.myautismteam.com/resources/temple-grandin-on-the-importance-of-giving-kids-with-autism-a-50-s-upbringing

Myers, I. B., McCaulley, M. H., Quenk, N. L., & Hammer, A. L. (1998/2003). *MBTI manual: A guide to the development and use of the Myers-Briggs Type Indicator* (3rd ed.). Palo Alto, CA: Consulting Psychologists Press.

Myles, B. S., Aspy, R., Mataya, K., & Shaffer, H. (2017). *Deliberate practice and critical mass: Excelling with autism across the lifespan.* Future Horizons

Myles, B. S., Mahler, K., & Robbins, L. (2016). *Sensory issues and high-functioning autism and related disorders. Practical solutions for making sense of the world.* Future Horizons.

Myles, B. S., & Simpson, R. L. (2001). Understanding the hidden curriculum: An essential social skill for children and youth with Asperger Syndrome. *Intervention in School and Clinic, 36,* 279-286.

Myles, B. S., Trautman, M., & Schelvan, R. L. (2013). *The hidden curriculum: for understanding unstated rules in social situations for adolescents and young adults.* Future Horizons.

National Professional Development Center on Autism Spectrum Disorders (NPDC). (2011). *Evidence-based practices.* Retrieved from http://autismpdc.fpg.unc.edu

Odom, S., L., McConnell, S. R., & McEvoy, M. A. (1992). *Social competence of young children with disabilities: Issues and strategies for intervention.* Baltimore, MD: Paul H. Brookes.

Petrie, D. (Director). (2003). *How to lose a guy in 10 days* [Motion Picture]. Los Angeles, CA: Paramount Pictures.

Prizant, B. M., & Fields-Meyer, T. (2015). *Uniquely human: A different way of seeing autism.* New York, NY: Simon & Schuster.

Quill, K. A. (1997). Instructional considerations for young children with autism: The rationale for visually cued instruction. *Journal of Autism and Developmental Disorders, 27,* 697-714.

Quinn, M. M., Kavale, K. A., Mathur, S. R., Rutherford Jr., R. B., & Forness, S. R. (1999). A meta-analysis of social skills interventions for students with emotional and behavioral disorders. *Journal of Emotional and Behavioral Disorders, 7,* 54-64.

Radley, K. C., Roderick, D. O., Ness, E. J., Ford, W. B., Battaglia, A. A., McHugh, M. B., & McLemore, C. E. (2014). Promoting social skill use and generalization in children with autism spectrum disorder. *Research in Autism Spectrum Disorders, 8,* 669-680.

Rao, P., Beidel, D., & Murray, M. (2008). Social skills interventions for children with Asperger's Syndrome and high functioning autism: A review and recommendations. *Journal of Autism and Developmental Disorders, 38,* 353-361.

Reaven, J., & Hepburn, S. (2003). Cognitive-behavioral treatment of obsessive compulsive disorder in a child with Asperger syndrome. *Autism, 7,* 145-164.

Risch, N., Hoffman, T. J., Anderson, M., Croen, L. A., Grether, J. K., & Windham, G. C. (2014). Familial recurrence of autism spectrum disorder: Evaluating genetic and environmental contributions. *The American Journal of Psychiatry, 171,* 1206-1213.

Sasso, G. M., Mundschenk, N. A., Melloy, K. J., & Casey, S. D. (1998). A comparison of the effects of organismic and setting variables on the social interaction behavior of children with developmental disabilities and autism. *Focus on Autism and Other Developmental Disabilities, 13*(1), 2-16.

Seaman, A. M. (2012, September 3). Almost half of teens with autism bullied: Study. *Chicago Tribune.* Retrieved from http://articles.chicagotribune.com/2012-09-03/lifestyle/sns-rt-us-teen-autismbre8820lg-20120903_1_autism-spectrum-disorder-asperger-autistic-children

Seinfeld, J. (2002). *Halloween.* Boston, MA: Little, Brown and Company.

Sheridan, M. (2010). *The tough kid social skills book.* Eugene, OR: Pacific Northwest Publishing.

Sherman, J., Rasmussen, C., & Baydala, L. (2008). The impact of teacher factors and behavioral outcomes for children with attention deficit/hyperactivity disorder (ADHD): A review of the literature. *Educational Research, 50,* 347-360.

Smith, L. E., Barker, E. T., Seltzer, M. M., Abbeduto, L, & Greenberg, J. S. (2012). Behavioral phenotype of fragile X syndrome in adolescence and adulthood. *American Journal on Intellectual and Developmental Disabilities, 117*(1), 1-17.

Smith, M., & Segal, J. (2016, October). *Laughter is the best medicine.* Retrieved from http://www.helpguide.org/articles/emotional-health/laughter-is-the-best-medicine.htm

Sofronoff, K., Dark, E., & Stone, V. (2011). Social vulnerability and bullying in children with Asperger syndrome. *Autism, 15*(3), 355-372.

Stichter, J. P., Conroy, M. A., & Kauffman, J. M. (2007). *An introduction to students with high incidence disabilities.* Upper Saddle River, NJ: Prentice Hall.

Stichter, J. P., O'Connor, K. V., Herzog, M. J., Lierheimer, K., & McGhee, S. D. (2012). Social competence intervention for elementary students with Aspergers Syndrome and high functioning autism. *Journal of Autism and Developmental Disorders, 42,* 354-366. doi:10.1007/s10803-011-1249-2

Stichter, J. P., Randolph, J., Gage, N., & Schmidt, C. (2007). A review of recommended social competency programs for students with autism spectrum disorders. *Exceptionality, 15,* 219-232.

Storey, K., Bates, P., McGhee, N., & Dycus, S. (1984). Reducing the self-stimulatory behavior of a profoundly retarded female through sensory awareness training. *American Journal of Occupational Therapy, 38,* 510-516.

Strain, P. S., & Odom, S. L. (1986). Peer social initiations: An effective intervention for social skill deficits of preschool handicapped children. *Exceptional Children, 52,* 543-552.

Timler, G. R., Vogler-Elias, D., & McGill, K. F. (2007). Strategies for promoting generalization of social communication skills in preschoolers and school-aged children. T*opics in Language Disorders, 27*(2), 167-181.

Uzgiris, I. C. (1981). Two functions of imitation during infancy. *International Journal of Behavioral Development, 4*(1), 1-12.

Wagner, T. (2008). *The global achievement gap.* New York, NY: Basic Books.

Walker, V. (2013). *Becoming aware: A text/workbook for human relations and personal development.* Dubuque, IA: Kendall Hunt Publishing Company.

Wheeler, J. J., & Carter, S. L. (1998). Using visual cues in the classroom for learners with autism as a method for promoting positive behavior. *B.C. Journal of Special Education, 21,* 64-73.

Wilson, K. (2013). Incorporating video modeling into a school-based intervention for students with autism spectrum disorders. *Language, Speech, and Hearing Services in Schools, 44,* 105-117.

Winner, M. G. (2000). *Inside out: What makes a person with social cognitive deficits tick?* San Jose, CA: Think Social Publishing.

Winner, M. G. (2007). *Thinking about you, thinking about me.* San Jose, CA: Think Social Publishing.

Winner, M. G. (2009). *Socially curious, curiously social.* San Jose, CA: Think Social Publishing.

Yaffe, P. (2011). The 7% rule: Fact, fiction, or misunderstanding. *Ubiquity,* October, 1-5. doi:10.1145/2043155.2043156

Yakubova, G., & Taber-Doughty, T. (2013). Effects of video modeling and prompting on social skills embedded within a purchasing activity for students with autism. *Journal of Special Education Technology, 28,* 35-47.

Zablotsky, B., Bradshaw, C. P., Anderson, C. M., & Law, P. (2014). Risk factors for bullying among children with autism spectrum disorders. *Autism, 18*(4), 419-427.

Zeldin, A. L., Britner, S. L., & Pajares, F. (2008). A comparative study of the self-efficacy beliefs of successful men and women in mathematics, science, and technology careers. *Journal of Research in Science Teaching, 45*(9), 1036-1058.

APPENDICES

APPENDIX 1

Autism Social Skills Profile

Scott Bellini

Child's Name: _____

Birthdate: _____ Age: _____ Sex: ☐Female ☐Male Today's Date: _____

School: _____ Grade: _____

Your Name: _____

Relationship to Child: ☐Mother ☐Father ☐Guardian ☐Other _____

Street Address: _____

City: _____ State: _____ Zip: _____

Phone: (_____) _____

The following phrases describe skills or behaviors that your child might exhibit during social interactions or in social situations. Please rate **HOW OFTEN** your child exhibits each skill or behavior independently, **without assistance from others** (i.e., without reminders, cueing and/or prompting). You should base your judgment on your child's behavior over the last **3 months**.

Please use the following guidelines to rate your child's behavior:

Circle **N** if your child **never** or **almost never** exhibits the skill or behavior.

Circle **S** if your child **sometimes** or **occasionally** exhibits the skill or behavior.

Circle **O** if your child **often** or **typically** exhibits the skill or behavior.

Circle **V** if your child **very often** or **always** exhibits the skill or behavior.

Please do not skip any items. If you are unsure of an item, please provide your best estimate. You may use the "Brief Description" section to provide additional information on the particular skill or behavior. For instance, if your child will exhibit a particular skill or behavior more frequently when cueing or prompting is provided, or when interacting with adults rather than peers, please make note of this in the "Brief Description" section.

From Bellini, S. (2006). *Building social relationships: A systematic approach to teaching social interaction skills to children and adolescents with autism spectrum disorders and other social difficulties.* Shawnee Mission, KS: Autism Asperger Publishing Co. Reprinted with permission.

Autism Social Skills Profile

Never	Sometimes	Often	Very often
N	S	O	V

Skill Area	How Often				Brief Description
Invites Peers to Join Him/Her in Activities	N 1	S 2	O 3	V 4	
Joins in Activities With Peers	N 1	S 2	O 3	V 4	
Takes Turns During Games and Activities	N 1	S 2	O 3	V 4	
Maintains Personal Hygiene	N 1	S 2	O 3	V 4	
Interacts With Peers During Unstructured Activities	N 1	S 2	O 3	V 4	
Interacts With Peers During Structured Activities	N 1	S 2	O 3	V 4	
Asks Questions to Request Information About a Person	N 1	S 2	O 3	V 4	
Asks Questions to Request Information About a Topic	N 1	S 2	O 3	V 4	
Engages in One-On-One Social Interactions With Peers	N 1	S 2	O 3	V 4	
Interacts With Groups of Peers	N 1	S 2	O 3	V 4	
Maintains the "Give-and-Take" of Conversations	N 1	S 2	O 3	V 4	
Expresses Sympathy for Others	N 1	S 2	O 3	V 4	
Talks About or Acknowledges the Interests of Others	N 1	S 2	O 3	V 4	

From Bellini, S. (2006). *Building social relationships: A systematic approach to teaching social interaction skills to children and adolescents with autism spectrum disorders and other social difficulties.* Shawnee Mission, KS: Autism Asperger Publishing Co. Reprinted with permission.

Autism Social Skills Profile

Never	Sometimes	Often	Very often
N	S	O	V

Skill Area	How Often				Brief Description
Recognizes the Facial Expressions of Others	N 1	S 2	O 3	V 4	
Recognizes the Nonverbal Cues, or "Body Language" of Others	N 1	S 2	O 3	V 4	
Requests Assistance From Others	N 1	S 2	O 3	V 4	
Understands the Jokes or Humor of Others	N 1	S 2	O 3	V 4	
Maintains Eye Contact During Conversations	N 1	S 2	O 3	V 4	
Maintains an Appropriate Distance When Interacting With Peers	N 1	S 2	O 3	V 4	
Speaks With an Appropriate Volume in Conversations	N 1	S 2	O 3	V 4	
Considers Multiple Viewpoints	N 1	S 2	O 3	V 4	
Offers Assistance to Others	N 1	S 2	O 3	V 4	
Verbally Expresses How He/She Is Feeling	N 1	S 2	O 3	V 4	
Responds to the Greetings of Others	N 1	S 2	O 3	V 4	
Joins a Conversation With Two or More People Without Interrupting	N 1	S 2	O 3	V 4	
Initiates Greetings With Others	N 1	S 2	O 3	V 4	

From Bellini, S. (2006). *Building social relationships: A systematic approach to teaching social interaction skills to children and adolescents with autism spectrum disorders and other social difficulties.* Shawnee Mission, KS: Autism Asperger Publishing Co. Reprinted with permission.

Autism Social Skills Profile

Never	Sometimes	Often	Very often
N	S	O	V

Skill Area	How Often				Brief Description
Provides Compliments to Others	N 1	S 2	O 3	V 4	
Introduces Self to Others	N 1	S 2	O 3	V 4	
Politely Asks Others to Move out of His/Her Way	N 1	S 2	O 3	V 4	
Acknowledges the Compliments Directed at Him/Her by Others	N 1	S 2	O 3	V 4	
Allows Peers to Join Him/Her in Activities	N 1	S 2	O 3	V 4	
Responds to the Invitations of Peers to Join Them in Activities	N 1	S 2	O 3	V 4	
Allows Others to Assist Him/Her With Tasks	N 1	S 2	O 3	V 4	
Responds to Questions Directed at Him/Her by Others	N 1	S 2	O 3	V 4	
Experiences Positive Peer Interactions	N 1	S 2	O 3	V 4	
Compromises During Disagreements With Others	N 1	S 2	O 3	V 4	
Responds Slowly in Conversations	N 1	S 2	O 3	V 4	
Changes the Topic of Conversation to Fit Self-Interests	N 1	S 2	O 3	V 4	
Misinterprets the Intentions of Others	N 1	S 2	O 3	V 4	

Never	Sometimes	Often	Very often
N	S	O	V

Skill Area	How Often				Brief Description
Makes Inappropriate Comments	N 1	S 2	O 3	V 4	
Engages in Solitary Interests and Hobbies	N 1	S 2	O 3	V 4	
Ends Conversations Abruptly	N 1	S 2	O 3	V 4	
Fails to Read Cues to Terminate Conversations	N 1	S 2	O 3	V 4	
Exhibits Fear or Anxiety Regarding Social Interactions	N 1	S 2	O 3	V 4	
Experiences Negative Peer Interactions	N 1	S 2	O 3	V 4	
Engages in Socially Inappropriate Behaviors	N 1	S 2	O 3	V 4	
Exhibits Poor Timing With His/Her Social Initiations	N 1	S 2	O 3	V 4	
Is Manipulated by Peers	N 1	S 2	O 3	V 4	
Engages in Solitary Activities in the Presence of Peers	N 1	S 2	O 3	V 4	

From Bellini, S. (2006). *Building social relationships: A systematic approach to teaching social interaction skills to children and adolescents with autism spectrum disorders and other social difficulties.* Shawnee Mission, KS: Autism Asperger Publishing Co. Reprinted with permission.

APPENDIX 2
IEP GOALS

Please note: The PEERspective data collection sheets in Appendix 1 and Appendix 5 are useful tools for gathering data on many of the following IEP goals across different settings.

Conversation Skills

- In the resource room, _____will independently initiate, maintain, and terminate reciprocal conversations with a peer at least once a day, 4 days a week.

- When engaging in conversations with his peers,_____will talk about topics unrelated to his area of interest 3 out of 4 times observed.

- In the resource room,_____will independently demonstrate all 5 steps in Body Basics (face the other person, use eye contact, appropriate voice, expression matching what is being said, look relaxed) at least twice daily 4 out of 5 school days.

- _____will independently initiate, maintain and terminate reciprocal conversations with peers in the general classroom setting once a day 2 times a week.

- _____will initiate a conversation with a peer without prompting at least 3 times a week in 3 out of 5 of his general education classes.

- _____will be able to identify at least 4 categories of topics used to initiate conversational language.

- _____will be able to use 1 of the 4 conversation categories previously brainstormed to initiate a reciprocal conversation with an adult in the school community___ times a week.

- _____will be able to use 1 of the 4 conversation categories previously brainstormed to initiate a reciprocal conversation with a peer in the school community___times a week.

Authentic Social Skill Practice

- _____will participate in at least 4 out of 5 PLA field trips and extracurricular activities through the school year.

- _____will independently ask a sales clerk a question and/or order his own meal on social outings associated with PEERspective or Social Communication Club (SCC).

Perspective Taking

- _____will continue to enhance his social awareness and/or theory of mind (TOM) by recording social situations and meeting with her special education teacher at least once a week for 10 minutes to discuss these situations.

- _____will be able to identify at least 4 categories of topics used to initiate conversational language.

- _____will keep a word document on his computer of thoughts he would like to say but decides not to.

- _____will be able to list at least 2 thoughts that someone may have in the social situation being discussed with his special education teacher.
- _____will categorize the social situations he records into the categories of "can" and "can't" control and/or "big problem" and "little problem" (e.g., gossip, cursing in the hallway, peers joking with each other.

Group Work and Joining In

- In the general classroom setting, _____will independently select a study partner or join a group of peers without prompting 3 out of 5 opportunities.
- In a resource room or general classroom setting,_____will join an ongoing conversation between his peers at least twice a week.
- In the resource room,_____will recognize and demonstrate the ability to use verbal and non-verbal language to demonstrate interest in her peers, 4 out of 5 opportunities.
- _____will convey to others an interest in interacting socially through his facial expressions, vocal intonation, and body language 3 out of 5 times during PEERspective activities.
- _____will convey to others an interest in interacting socially through his facial expressions, vocal intonation, and body language 3 out of 5 times during structured and unstructured activities throughout the school community.
- _____will initiate and maintain a reciprocal conversation with a peer through 3 exchanges by asking questions, providing acknowledging comments, or giving a compliment, 4 out of 5 days a week.

Other Areas

- _____will raise his hand for permission to speak, 3 out of 4 times in all of his general classes.
- When given a long-term assignment, _____will break up the assignment into 3-5 smaller assignments and assign intermittent deadlines, resulting in the project being completed at least 1 day before the due date.
- _____will independently organize his binders by placing all papers in the appropriate locations at least once a week.
- Whenever possible, _____will turn in his assignments electronically either through e-mail or a web-based system.
- _____will make no more than 3 remarks (questions or comments) during a 50-minute class period.
- _____will mark on his comment card each time he makes a comment or asks a question, no more than 3 remarks each class period.
- _____will show awareness of his body placement by staying about an arm's length away from others when moving through the school community.
- _____will show awareness of proximity by maintaining about an arm's length distance when asking a question, making a comment, and/or having a conversation.

From Schmidt, J. Why didn't they just say that? Teaching secondary students with high-functioning autism to decode the social world using PEERspective. ©2018 Jennifer Schmidt. Published by Future Horizons. Used with permission.

APPENDIX 3
Sample Proposal to Administration
PEERSpective

This proposal is to teach a yearlong class to students with social skills deficits at the high school. Completion of the class will earn students one credit towards graduation. The class will be taught during the lunch period to allow the students to practice supervised socialization in an authentic setting. This class would include skills outlined in the human relations curriculum.

Rationale

We have many students with social communication deficits in the high school. Many have been diagnosed with high-functioning autism or social communication disorder. Some of these students have IEPs for speech language services, as well as tutoring from a special educator. At times, they do not work as well as their peers in groups when assigned to participate with others on a collaborative assignment. Many of these students eat alone at lunch and do not socialize as well as their peers. Finally, these students often are targets for bullying or unknowingly make inappropriate comments at school that get them into trouble.

Units

Unit 1 – Trust and Teambuilding

Unit 2 – Self-Awareness, Self-Acceptance, Self-Disclosure

Unit 3 – Relationships

Unit 4 – Conflict Resolution

Unit 5 – Communication Skills

Unit 6 – Stress Management

Unit 7 – Social Etiquette

Unit 8 – Life Transitions

Class Structure

The class should be held in a room near the lunchroom for easy access to observe and participate in group situations.

The class will consist of:

1. Instruction

2. Discussion

3. Practice/role-play

4. Application of conversation rules during lunch

5. Social games to practice the skills taught

6. Projects and other activities to practice working as a group and making friends using appropriate socialization skills

7. Field trips/outings: One field trip (during school) and one outing (after school) each quarter to practice skills in authentic high school-age settings

APPENDIX 4
PEERSpective Syllabus

COURSE DESCRIPTION/PURPOSE

This course provides students with an understanding of human behavior. Interpersonal skill development is incorporated to help students recognize and enhance skills that are essential for building and maintaining relationships. To develop these skills, students are encouraged to share their ideas, thoughts, and feelings with their peers, as well as participate in group-interaction activities in authentic settings. Each quarter we will have a guest speaker, a field trip, and outside activities to further understanding of topics discussed in class. These activities will also allow students to practice socializing in appropriate ways. In order to meet these goals, students must enhance their interpersonal skills that are essential for building and maintaining relationships including trust, communication, acceptance, and conflict resolution.

COURSE TOPICS

- Trust and Teambuilding
- Self-Awareness, Self-Acceptance, Disclosure
- Relationships
- Conflict Resolution
- Communication Skills
- Stress Management
- Social Etiquette
- Life Transitions

TEXT; each student will be provided a copy as needed in class.

Walker, V. (2013). *Becoming aware: A text/workbook for human relations and personal adjustment* (12th ed.). Dubuque, IA: Kendall/Hunt.

REQUIREMENTS FOR STUDENT ASSIGNMENTS

1. Attendance and participation:
   Since this course is based on building interpersonal skills, it is important that you come to class and participate on a regular basis. Most of your grade will be based on participation in group activities and group discussions; therefore, absences will severely hurt your grade.

2. The following items are needed for class:
   a. A notebook and folder for journal assignments
   b. Pen or pencil

GRADING POLICY

The school grading scale will be used.
Adding the total number of points earned and dividing them by the total number of points possible will average your grades.

TOTAL EARNED/TOTAL POSSIBLE = PERCENTAGE GRADE

APPENDIX 5
Sample Form for Teachers to Complete to Identify Potential Student Participants

PEERspective Data Collection Sheet

Student's Name_____   Date_____

Evaluator_____

During the observed class period please track the number of times each below behavior occurs:

_____ Joins in the activity with his/her peers without prompting

_____ Maintains eye contact when speaking or listening

_____ Speaks with appropriate volume in conversations

_____ Initiates greetings with others

_____ Maintains appropriate distance when interacting with others

_____ Considers others' opinions

_____ Stays on topic

_____ Smiles at peers/teacher at appropriate times

# of times above behaviors were demonstrated in a _____ minute group activity
     = _____

Anecdotal Summary of Observation

APPENDIX 6
Sample Letter for Parents of Targeted Students

Dear Parents,

Your child has been chosen to be a part of PEERspective. This class is a human relations course with a special focus on communication skills. While taking this course, your child will learn social skills needed to communicate more effectively. All students in this course will be held to the standards of the human relations curriculum. Your child has been chosen because he/she could benefit from intentional social skill training. The topics we will cover include: trust and teambuilding, self-awareness, self-acceptance, disclosure, relationships, conflict resolution, communication skills, stress management, social etiquette, and life transitions.

With your permission, the counselors will adjust your child's schedule to include this class. Your child will earn one elective credit towards graduation for the year in the class, and will be expected to take part in all assignments and activities. The class will include peer coaches who have been hand selected and trained to be social models while taking the course.

_____

Please include my child,_____, in PEERspective for the upcoming school year. I understand that the counselor will adjust my child's previously scheduled class to reflect this placement. I also understand that my child will earn one elective credit towards graduation after successful completion of the course.

Parent Signature_____ Date_____

Student Agreement

I am interested in being enrolled in PEERspective.

Student Signature_____ Date_____

Sample Letter for Parents of Potential Peer Coaches

Dear Parents,
Your child has been chosen to be a peer coach for PEERspective. This class is a human relations course with a special focus on communication skills. While taking this course, your child will serve as a social model for other students who are learning to communicate more effectively. All students in this course will participate in a human relations curriculum utilizing a college-level textbook.

Some of the students in the class have been diagnosed with high-functioning autism (formerly known as Asperger Syndrome). While these students are in mostly regular to advanced classes, they struggle with everyday communication in social situations. Your child has been chosen because he/she exhibits strong social skills, character, empathy, and works easily with a variety of students. Each of our peer coaches have been hand-selected for this important role. Many have already worked with their peers with communication difficulties and have shown great compassion and patience, and the class would not be as effective without their participation.

_____

With your permission, the counselors will call your child down to the office to adjust his/her schedule. As a peer coach, your child will earn one elective credit towards graduation, and will be expected to take part in all assignments and activities.

We will be holding an important one-day training session for all peer coaches. This session will cover characteristics of autism and train the students to be effective peer coaches. Failure to attend the training will result in dropping this class.

Please include my child, _____, as a peer coach for PEERspective. I understand that the counselor will call him/her into the office to adjust previously scheduled classes to reflect this placement. I also understand that my child will earn one elective credit towards graduation.

Parent Signature_____Date_____

Peer Coach Agreement

I am interested in being a peer coach for PEERspective, and I am willing to attend the training session over the summer. I understand that I will be taking the course as well as coaching my peers on effective communication strategies.

Student Signature_____Date_____

APPENDIX 7
PEERspective Checklist

☐ Research the number of students with autism in your building/district who are high functioning.

☐ Send out data collection sheets for each of your prospective target students to one or more of their teachers.

☐ Write a proposal to the administrator about setting up a program and include sample letter(s) to parents, as well as syllabus.

☐ Set up a meeting with your building principal and/or special education supervisor.

☐ Send out letters to both peer coaches and targeted students.

☐ Hold two informational meetings; one for peer coaches and one for targeted students.

APPENDIX 8
PEER COACH TRAINING AGENDA

1. Introductions/getting-to-know-you activity

2. Journal: What do you know about autism spectrum disorders? What do you need to know in order to be an effective peer coach?

3. Video training part one (peerspectivelearningapproach.com)

4. 10-minute break

5. Video training part two (peerspectivelearningapproach.com)

6. Former peer coach panel

7. Lunch (provided)

8. Former parent perspective

9. 10-minute break

10. Simulation activity: How it feels to have autism

11. Wrapup & dismissal

APPENDIX 9
SAMPLE MALL SCAVENGER HUNT FIELD TRIP ACTIVITY

Names:_____   Date:_____

Ask the following questions at each bolded location, practicing appropriate communication skills at all times.

Guest Services
1. How do you rent a stroller?

Great American Cookie
1. How much advance time do you need to personalize (put a name on it for someone's birthday for example) a cookie? What does the length of time depend on?

T-Mobile
1. What is the newest phone you offer? How much is it?

Icing/Claire's
1. Who has the best price for a basic ear piercing?

JC Penney
1. (Salon) How much is a child's haircut?

Game Stop
1. What gaming system do you like best?
2. Do you have the XBOX 1 in stock?

Chick-Fil-A
1. What are two items not available at this Chick-Fil-A location that are also available at other stores?

F.Y.E.
1. Do you have Bluetooth speakers? Can I use that with my phone? (Tell them what phone you have.)

Fetch
1. Do you have pets that are non-allergic? If so, list the types.

Hickory Farm (kiosk)
1. Can you ship to Hawaii? Does it cost extra? What is the procedure?

Avoiding people trying to sell you things or give free samples:

- 3 points if you get past them without making eye contact or talking with them.
- 2 points if you have to say "no thank you" and walk away.
- 0 points if you take a sample or let them try to talk you into something.

Did you encounter any of these people? _____

How did you do? Grade yourself. _____points

The scavenger hunt is not based on time. I will be observing your communication skills, and checking the answers for accuracy. You will have one hour to answer as many of the above as possible. Your answer does not count if you don't ask the question.

APPENDIX 10
BOOK DISCUSSION LOG

Name_____ Period_____

My Book Discussion Ideas

Book Title: _____ Chapters: _____

What I thought was applicable to my life:

What I didn't agree with or didn't understand:

Takeaways from this chapter:

I relate to this, how:

Quotes: (use page numbers):

APPENDIX 11
BOOK DISCUSSION PARTNER ASSESSMENT

Name_____

Partner's Name_____

Date_____

_____(1) Takeaway

_____(1) Comment or question

_____(1) Quote from the text

5 points each for a total of 15 points

_____/15

Teacher Comments:

APPENDIX 12
Comment Card

☐ Comment #1

☐ Comment #2

☐ Comment #3

You are finished for this class period. Please keep it in your "Thought Bubble"

☐ Comment #1

☐ Comment #2

☐ Comment #3

You are finished for this class period. Please keep it in your "Thought Bubble"

☐ Comment #1

☐ Comment #2

☐ Comment #3

You are finished for this class period. Please keep it in your "Thought Bubble"

☐ Comment #1

☐ Comment #2

☐ Comment #3

You are finished for this class period. Please keep it in your "Thought Bubble"

☐ Comment #1

☐ Comment #2

☐ Comment #3

You are finished for this class period. Please keep it in your "Thought Bubble"

☐ Comment #1

☐ Comment #2

☐ Comment #3

You are finished for this class period. Please keep it in your "Thought Bubble"

APPENDIX 13
CURRICULUM MAP

1st Quarter:

- ✓ Request information about your students on the spectrum from general education teachers around week 3. Use *Bellini Social Skills Profile*. This will give you baseline data regarding their social skills.
- ✓ Pretest
- ✓ Unit 1, Unit 2 (Chapters 5 and 6 in *Becoming Aware*)
- ✓ 1 Experts for a Day project
- ✓ 1 outing, 1 field trip
- ✓ Chapters 1-3 in *Socially Curious, Curiously Social* (Winner, 2009) with a book talk

2nd Quarter:

- ✓ Unit 3, Unit 4 (Chapters 7 and 8 in *Becoming Aware*)
- ✓ 1 Experts for a Day project
- ✓ 1 outing, 1 field trip
- ✓ Chapters 4-6 in *Socially Curious, Curiously Social* (Winner, 2009) with a Book Talk
- ✓ Midterm assessment (practical exam on stress management)

3rd Quarter:

- ✓ Unit 5, Unit 6 (Chapters 9 and 10 in *Becoming Aware*)
- ✓ 1 Experts for a Day project
- ✓ 1 outing, 1 field trip
- ✓ Chapters 7-9 in *Socially Curious, Curiously Social* (Winner, 2009) with a Book Talk

4th Quarter:

- ✓ Unit 7 and Unit 8 (Chapters 11 and 12 in *Becoming Aware*)
- ✓ 1 Experts for a Day project
- ✓ 1 outing, 1 field trip
- ✓ Chapters 10-13 in *Socially Curious, Curiously Social* (Winner, 2009) with a Book Talk
- ✓ Final Exam (mock interview)
- ✓ Posttest and class evaluation
- ✓ Request post-class information from general education teachers; use Bellini Social Skills Profile

MORE PRAISE FOR *"WHY DIDN'T THEY JUST SAY THAT?"*

"Every middle and high school should offer a class like PEERspective! Sharing examples from real PEERspective students with autism and their neurotypical peers, Schmidt shows the positive impact a program like this will have on your students. The detailed curriculum includes goals and user-friendly lessons to help teachers and therapists design their class."

> – Amy Moore Gaffney, MA, CCC-SLP, speech-language pathologist, autism consultant for public and nonpublic schools in Indianapolis, Indiana

"'Why Didn't They Just Say That?' is a practical guide to creating and delivering meaningful social skills instruction for students with high-functioning autism. The step-by-step PEERspective curriculum lays out why and how to included neurotypical peers so that skills can be learned and generalized across settings; besides, it is easy to follow and adapt to the individual needs of all students and programs, including how to propose a social skills class to school administration, setting up social outings, and much more This is a must-have resource for anybody charged with designing social skills programs that are relevant, enthusiastic, and doable."

> – Elisa Gagnon, MsEd, behavior support teacher; author of *The Power Card Strategy 2.0: Using Special Interests to Motivate Children and Youth With Autism Spectrum Disorder*

"This curriculum has been created from a place of genuine respect, understanding, and sensitivity to the diverse strengths and needs of students with social communication challenges. Well organized, practical, entertaining, and insightful, this book comes 'ready to implement' and 'ready to change lives.'"

> – Lisa Combs, MA, CAS, special education consultant, author, and university instructor; author of *Push to Open: A Teacher's QuickGuide to Universal Design for Teaching Students on the Autism Spectrum in the General Education Classroom* and coauthor of *Gear up for Success: A Three-Tiered Planning Model for Supporting Learners on the Autism Spectrum*

CPSIA information can be obtained
at www.ICGtesting.com
Printed in the USA
JSHW062034170723
44950JS00002B/2